Retiring Well

by Hope Egan
Matthew James
Barbara Wagner

Formerly published as
Barnes & Noble Basics Retiring
and Barnes & Noble Basics Using your PC

BARNES
& NOBLE
B O O K S
NEW YORK

Substantial portions of this book were originally published in 2003 as **Barnes & Noble Basics** *Retiring* and **Barnes & Noble Basics** *Using your PC*

Printed and bound in the United States of America.

For information, contact:
Barnes & Noble, Inc.
122 Fifth Avenue
New York, NY 10011
212-633-4000

introduction

"I can't believe it, I am finally retiring!" exclaimed my friend Elaine. "All I want to do is sleep late and read the paper from cover to cover—but I think I need to see my accountant first thing in the morning because I'm getting really nervous about my money. How do I take it out? How much should I take out? To say nothing of my really big concern: Will my money last me? Why does it all have to be so nerve-racking?"

Doing anything new can bring on a case of the nerves. And since retiring is a new phase of your life, it's natural to be a tad concerned. But not a nervous wreck. That's why we came up with *Retiring Well*. It has all you need to know, from planning your retirement budget to deciding where to live, not to mention how exactly to get Social Security and Medicare. It's both calming and smart. And there's no financial jargon, no worrisome charts and forms. Just the basics, pure and simple, and in plain English. You'll learn how easy it is to get a reverse mortgage and organize your finances. Plus, you'll get the inside track on travel for seniors (lots of neat ways to see the world) and health do's and don'ts.

So start reading. Your retirement is going to be a lot more fun than you expected.

Barb Chintz
Editorial Director, the **Barnes & Noble Basics**™ Series

table of contents

your *money*

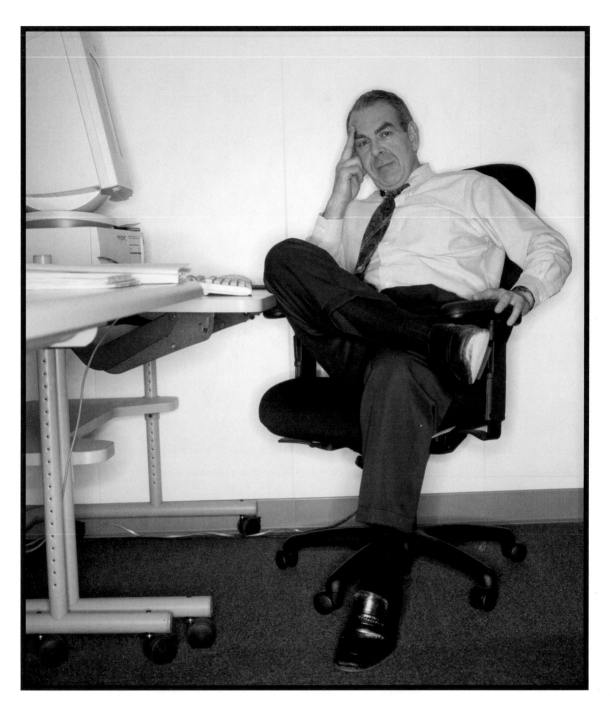

I've been meaning to get my finances in order for years. Am I too late?

get your *finances* in order

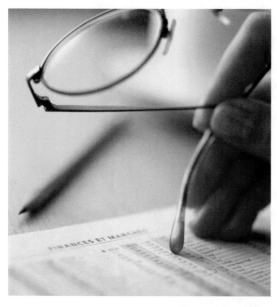

Know what you've got

YOU'VE WAITED FOR RETIREMENT for many years, and now it's here—finally! In case you're feeling a little nervous about the financial part of it, relax, it's normal. All major life transitions usually involve some sort of financial review, and retirement is no exception. Whatever you do, don't let money concerns or fears keep you from enjoying this exciting phase of life. Knowing exactly where you are with regard to your money will help answer all your questions, such as "Will my savings last as long as I do? Should I sell the house? How much travel can I afford? Should I work part time to supplement my income?"

And don't be too hard on yourself: They didn't teach retirement planning in school. So if going over your finances seems really daunting, don't fret. You can always hire a financial planner to help you get your finances in order and on the right track (see page 24 for information). But even if you do hire one, you should still have a basic understanding of your finances. So keep reading, and we'll show you what to do.

ASK THE EXPERTS

I didn't start saving for retirement until after I put all my kids through college; I just assumed my pension and Social Security would be enough. Will I be okay?

Many folks put their children through college before they start saving for retirement, so they don't have a lot of years to save before they actually retire. The key to retirement lies in your spending needs: How much do you need to live on? How much do you want on hand for trips or other postretirement activities or purchases? Even if you've never thought twice about retirement before, now's the time to have a plan.

I've been meaning to get my finances in order for years. Am I too late?

Not at all! There's plenty you can still do, even if you're already retired. During our working years, we all have good intentions about tracking our expenses or starting a budget, but few of us actually find the time. Retirement frees you up so you can finally tend to your personal finances. And it's especially important to do now, since the difference between living a full, happy retirement, and being afraid to spend any money, is often having a good plan.

I've figured that my pension and Social Security check will cover my expenses. Do I still need to plan?

Yes! Inflation and taxes can have a serious impact on your retirement if you haven't factored them into your plan. Keep reading—you might uncover some issues that don't impact you today but that you might need to consider down the road.

do you know how much *goes out?*

It's a relief to know for sure

THE BIGGEST FACTOR IN your financial plan—and the one you have the most control over—is your spending. It can be hard to measure. But the good news is that you don't need to figure it out to the exact penny; an estimate will do.

Why is it so important to start ballparking your expenses? Because when you were working, you probably had more than enough income to spend each month (even if it didn't always feel that way). With a reduced income that is often fixed, you'll have to pay attention to what goes out each month. Otherwise, you could run out of money.

There are many computer programs (like Quicken or Microsoft Money) that can help you track, as well as budget, your living expenses. If you're not up to that, simply start with good old-fashioned pencil and paper, and sketch out estimates of how much you spend each month. (See the example on the following page.) If you're not sure how much you spend in each category (most people aren't), try tracking all of your expenses for a few months in a little notebook. Once you observe your spending patterns and habits for a little while, it's easier to forecast your future expenditures.

As you estimate how much you'll need to live on when you are retired, you may find you'll spend money on entirely different things than you did while you were working (see the sidebar). Many people find that their expenses decrease by about 20 percent once they no longer have to go to work every day.

If you find that you have no clear idea of what you're spending, look at the sample spending sheet on the following page. It will help you track your expenses.

COMMON RETIREMENT SPENDING CHANGES

Typical increases
Health & medical

Entertainment, hobbies, travel

Telephone & utilities

Typical decreases
Clothing

Dry cleaning

Income taxes

Commuting/ parking

SAMPLE SPENDING SHEET

EXPENSE		MONTHLY	ANNUALLY
Fixed Expenses—You don't have much control over these			
Rent / Mortgage Payment			
Car Expenses:	Loan Payment		
	Fees and Licenses		
	Insurance		
Home Expenses:	Property Taxes		
	Condo Dues/Fees		
	Home Insurance		
Insurance:	Medical & Dental		
	Hospital		
	Long-term Care		
	Other		
TOTAL FIXED EXPENSES			
Variable Expenses—These you have some control over			
Car Expenses:	Gas		
	Repairs and Maintenance		
Clothing:	Apparel		
	Laundry and Dry Cleaning		
	Alterations and Shoe Repair		
Personal Expenses:	Toiletries		
	Health-club Dues		
Household Costs:	Decorating and Appliances		
	Repairs and Maintenance		
Utilities:	Gas and Electric		
	Water		
	Telephone/Cellular Phone/Pager		
	Cable		
	Computer and Internet		
Food:	Groceries		
	Restaurants		
Entertainment:	Hobbies		
	Travel		
	Books, Publications, Discs		
	Movies, Theater, Concerts		
Medical:	Doctors		
	Prescriptions		
	Vision		
	Dental		
Gifts and Charitable Donations			
Debt Payment			
Other			
TOTAL VARIABLE EXPENSES			
TOTAL ALL EXPENSES			

income and *assets*

How to spend your savings

OKAY, SO NOW YOU KNOW how much money you'll need to live on. Does it seem high? Relax. Before you panic, take a deep breath and see what resources you have to cover these expenses.

The ideal way is with **income**—cash flow that doesn't require you to dip into your retirement savings plans or other assets. This is money that will be coming to you, such as Social Security or your pension.

Your second line of defense is income from your **assets**—your 401(k) plans (page 94), IRAs and annuities (Chapter 7), and your other assets. If you need these assets to cover your regular living expenses, try limiting yourself to these assets' income (usually interest and dividends). For example, maybe you have a bond mutual fund that regularly pays 7 percent interest, which is then reinvested into the fund. Rather than selling part of the fund if you need extra money, don't reinvest the interest, but use it to live on. By leaving the **principal** (the main investment) untouched for as long as you can, you'll have it for the future.

There will come a time when you will need to go to your third line of defense—spending your assets' principal. After all, didn't you build up those assets in order to spend them during retirement? Keep in mind, however, that spending the principal can take on a life of its own—like a runaway train: the more you take out, the less income it'll provide, so the more you'll need to take out, etc. And depending on the asset, you may owe Uncle Sam capital gains tax on a portion of every sale (see page 226). If you're in a serious cash crunch, you might consider selling your home (page 48) or getting a reverse mortgage (page 46).

*t*hese are assets that you can sell to cover your living expenses. Make sure you write down the net amount—what you'd get after paying taxes or selling fees, or paying off any debt owed on the item.

SAMPLE INCOME SHEET

FIRST AND SECOND SOURCES OF INCOME
Social Security Income
Pension Income
Part-time or Consulting Work
Annuity Income
Dividend Income
Interest Income
Rental Income
Other Income

THIRD SOURCES OF INCOME
Savings/Money Market Accounts
Certificates of Deposit (CDs)
Stocks
Bonds
Mutual Funds
401(k)s
IRAs
SEPs or Keoghs
Rental Property
Home/Condo
Cash Value Life Insurance
Car(s)
Art, Antiques, Collectibles
Jewelry, Furs
Other Assets

what's the outlook *for you?*

It's an ongoing process

AFTER YOU'VE PULLED TOGETHER your spending total and compared it with your monthly income, how does it look? You'll generally come to one of the conclusions below.

● Your income and/or your plan for asset withdrawal far exceed your expenses. Congratulations! Your focus should be on estate planning (Chapter 12).

OR

● Your expenses closely match your income and/or asset withdrawal. In this case, spend some time fine-tuning your budget. First, make sure you've considered all of your regular and extraordinary expenses. Next, keep close tabs on what's coming in and going out, since inflation can gradually erode your buying power over time. Inflation causes your cost of living to increase, and if you're not paying attention, your expenses may eventually exceed your income. Then you might have to cut down on your living expenses.

OR

● Your expenses exceed your income and other assets. If this is the case, make your top priority cutting down on what you spend (see page 22). If that doesn't bring your expenses into line, you'll want to think about your living arrangements (see Chapter 3), since this is often the biggest expense folks have. You may be able to change your living arrangements enough to bring down your expenses. Or perhaps you can find additional sources of income, such as part-time employment. If there is a really big gap, you might need to reconsider your decision to retire.

ASK THE EXPERTS

I did a simple calculation, and things seem pretty good. Is there anything else I should do?

Good for you—all your planning paid off. That said, you need to continually review your finances. This is not a one-time exercise, it's a continuing process. Experts suggest you review your finances every month when you pay your bills. Why? Things change. For example, inflation could suddenly rise because gas prices rose or there could be changes in the stock market, your living situation, or your health. All these things and more could affect your financial stability. Try to keep on top of the changes.

I've tried to keep track of my expenses in the past, but I always seem to get overwhelmed. Any tips?

Start small. Tracking your expenses can indeed be overwhelming. But there's no reason to panic. You won't be able to track every single cup of coffee you buy or every newspaper you purchase. But don't let that keep you from trying. First, start collecting receipts from every purchase you make. Record these expenditures in a spending diary. As you write checks, make sure to write down the date, check number, payee, amount, and description of each. Then once or twice a month, sit down with your receipts, your diary, your check register, and your credit card statements to track what you've spent. If you're PC literate, consider compiling these in personal finance software (like Quicken).

investing during *retirement*

Inflation eats up "safe" investments

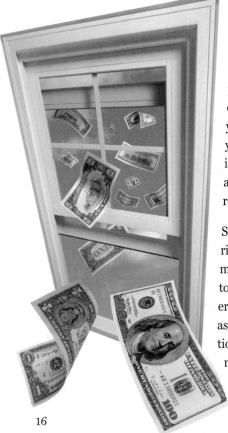

WHEN YOU WERE SAVING for retirement, you probably followed the traditional advice: Take some risk with stocks now while your retirement is far in the future, and you'll have time to weather the market's ups and downs. Well, your retirement is here—so now what?

Should you bail out of the stock market and put all of your money in a risk-free bank savings account? The answer is no, and the reason is inflation.

Inflation is that unstoppable increase in the cost of living as prices gradually go up. It's been averaging a relatively tame 3 percent or 4 percent over the past decade, so you probably didn't notice little day-to-day price increases in your milk, your clothes, or a pack of chewing gum. Applied over the years, and to bigger costs like rent, new cars, and furniture, inflation begins to add up. And the items in your budget with above-average inflation rates—health care and insurance—can really sting you.

Standard retirement investment advice once was: Shift your risky stock market assets to more stable, fixed-income investments, like bonds and CDs, as soon as you retire. But if you put too much of your savings in those stable assets, inflation will erode your savings. After all, your expenses keep rising, but your assets and income stay fixed or rise less than the rate of inflation. Keeping part of your savings exposed to prudent stock market investments where you are likely to see higher returns over time can help you hold your own against inflation.

ASK THE EXPERTS

I've done well with my retirement funds in the stock market over the years, even through economic ups and downs. So why should I make a change now?

As you know, like everything else in life, the stock market ebbs and flows. That's why investment diversification is so important, especially at this time in your life when financial security is so essential. Shifting part of your savings to more stable, fixed-income instruments will help protect your nest egg during the rough times while providing you with current income.

How much, exactly, should I keep in the market, and how much should I move to safer investments?

That's a great question. Deciding on your asset allocation (how much to invest in each category) is both an art and a science, and many professionals disagree over how to do it. Most financial planners calculate allocations based on your age, your risk tolerance, how much money you have, and how much money you need. Some professionals suggest an aggressive allocation of 60 percent stocks and 40 percent bonds for retirees who have a substantial nest egg. Other, more conservative planners suggest that, as a rule of thumb, retirees might match the percentage of their investment in bonds to their age. For example, if you are 65 years old, you might want about 65 percent of your savings in bonds; if you are 70, you might want about 70 percent in bonds, and so on.

how long will your *nest egg* last?

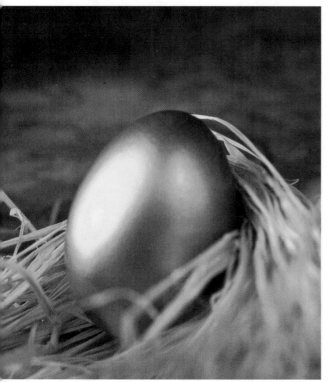

Making it last

IDEALLY, YOU WILL CONTINUE to invest during your retirement to help offset inflation. And, with luck, the interest and dividends you earn on those investments will serve you well. But chances are, sooner or later you may want to—or have to—start dipping into those investments. This is called spending down your **principal**.

After all, you did save it to spend during retirement. But spending principal requires planning so those assets will last as long as you'll need them. According to financial planners, it's a good idea to spend no more than 4.5 percent of your nest egg per year.

If you want to figure out the exact amount you'll need each year and you are computer-savvy, try using an electronic worksheet similar to the ones financial planners use, such as the one on the following page (furnished by T. Rowe Price free of charge on the Internet, see **www. troweprice.com/ retirement**). Another one can be found at **www. quicken.com**.

RETIREMENT PLANNING WORKSHEET

1. Enter your CURRENT SALARY (example: $30,000) $ [   ]

2. Enter your TAX RATE (example: 25%) [25% ▼]

3. Enter the estimated INFLATION RATE (example: 3%) [3% ▼]

4. Enter the number of YEARS until your retirement (example: 30) [   ]

5. Enter the number of YEARS you expect to live in retirement (example: 20) [   ]

6. Enter the PERCENT OF SALARY you need after retirement. A general rule of thumb is that you will need between 60% and 80% of your preretirement income to maintain your lifestyle (example: 70%) [70] %

7. Enter the RATE OF RETURN you expect to earn on your retirement savings after you retire. You might earn a lower rate of return after retirement, reflecting a more conservative investment strategy. You may wish to review historical returns for different investment categories (example: 6%) [6% ▼]

8. Enter any CURRENT INVESTMENTS in **taxable** accounts. Give a total number that includes your savings accounts, mutual funds, etc. (example: $20,000) $ [   ]

9. Enter the RATE OF RETURN you expect to earn on your current **taxable** investments between now and retirement. You may wish to consult historical returns (example: 8%) [8% ▼]

10. Enter your CURRENT ASSETS in **tax-deferred** accounts, including IRAs, 401(k)s, etc. (example: $50,000) $ [   ]

11. Enter your expected RATE OF RETURN on tax-deferred accounts before retirement, based on historical returns, if you wish (example: 8%) [8% ▼]

[Analyze]   [Reset]

This worksheet provides only an estimate based on the information you provide.

> Back to Top

paying taxes during *retirement*

How to pay Uncle Sam after you retire

JUST BECAUSE YOU'LL NO LONGER have withholding taxes taken out of a paycheck doesn't mean you won't owe taxes once you retire. What's more, Uncle Sam wants his tax money right away. You have two choices about how to pay. You can either make **estimated quarterly payments**—taxes you pay and send to the IRS every three months—or have your taxes **voluntarily withheld** from your monthly Social Security check, pension, and regular distributions from your IRA. If you don't do either of these, you will be hit with penalties when you file your annual return. (For Social Security withholding, simply file form W-4V or W-4P for pensions and 401(k)s and annuities. For your IRA, ask your broker for the proper form to fill out for voluntary withholding taxes.)

If you stop working (or cut down substantially), your income will no doubt be less. The good news is, you'll drop into a lower income tax bracket. That lower bracket can mean you owe less in taxes when you sell stock or withdraw money from retirement accounts. But some other investment strategies might change as a result. For example:

● You might want to pay off your mortgage, since your tax advantage on the interest may no longer be as attractive.
● Tax-exempt bonds (and their lower yields) are probably no longer a good investment choice for you. Consider looking for higher-yielding investments.

TAX CHANGES AND BREAKS THAT FAVOR SENIORS

HOME SALES A one-time profit of up to $500,000 ($250,000 if you're single) is not taxed if you meet certain requirements.

SOCIAL SECURITY Benefits are only partially taxable (see page 98).

STANDARD DEDUCTION The standard deduction increases for people 65 and older.

LIFE INSURANCE BENEFITS & INHERITANCES Proceeds from these windfalls are generally not taxed.

VETERANS' BENEFITS These are not subject to income tax.

PUBLIC ASSISTANCE Most financial aid for the elderly, such as winter energy subsidies, Nutrition Program for the Elderly, and other welfare programs, are not taxable.

CREDIT FOR THE ELDERLY If you're over 65 and your gross income is less than $17,500 ($25,000 if you're married filing jointly and you both qualify; $20,000 if one of you qualifies), you might be eligible for a tax credit of up to $1,125.

STATE INCOME TAXES Many states give additional tax exemptions to seniors. Some states also exclude retirement income like Social Security, pensions, and IRA withdrawals from taxation.

WHICH IRS PUBLICATIONS DO YOU NEED?

You can order IRS Publications by calling 800-TAX-FORM or download them from **www.irs.gov**.

Paying Quarterly Taxes	No. 505	Pension and Annuity Income	No. 575
Older Americans' Tax Guide	No. 554	Medical and Dental Expenses	No. 502
Social Security	No. 915		

REVISITING MEDICAL EXPENSES

Now's the time to take a look at medical bills. You can deduct medical expenses exceeding 7.5 percent of your income if you itemize. Some expenses that qualify (see IRS Publication 502 for more):

- Doctor fees
- Hospital costs
- Prescription drugs
- Eyeglasses and contacts
- Dental costs (including false teeth)
- Certain long-term care insurance premiums (see page 152)
- Medical insurance premiums, including
- Medicare Part B (see page 130)
- Hearing aids
- Crutches
- Wheelchairs
- Transportation to and from medical providers
- Certain medically related retirement home costs
- Health-related improvements to your home such as constructing wheelchair ramps, widening doorways, installing grab bars and railings or modifying stairs

money-saving *ideas*

Bargains take time to find— and time is what you have now

ARE YOU COST-CONSCIOUS? It's probably a habit you've meant to develop for years. But since your income may be decreasing now, it's a good time to start thinking about how you can cut costs. This is especially true if you have debts you're trying to pay off: The sooner you eliminate the interest that piles up each month, the sooner you can more fully enjoy your retirement.

Start with senior discounts. At 65, and sometimes as early as age 55, you can qualify for discounts on airfare, trains, hotels, car rentals, movies, and restaurants, just by asking. But you do have to ask, wherever you go (and be ready to show ID indicating your age). Most reservationists or cashiers won't give senior discounts without your prompting them. For even more senior spending clout, consider joining AARP, formerly known as the American Association of Retired Persons (see below). They provide members and their spouses with a wealth of information about bargains and discount services.

AARP (American Association of Retired Persons)

For only $10 a year, anyone over 50 can join. For more information, visit their Web site at **aarp.com**, call 800-424-3410, or e-mail member@aarp.org. You can also write them at: AARP, 601 E St. NW, Washington, DC 20049.

RED FLAG

Fewer working hours mean more hours available to Spend! Spend! Spend! Don't get caught in the spare-time spending trap, or you'll lose a hunk of money before your retirement really gets going.

COST-CUTTING IDEAS

- Transfer credit card balances to low-rate no-annual-fee cards. See **www.bankrate.com** or **www.bestrate.com** for a list of low-cost cards. Pay your balance in full every month to avoid interest.

- Learn to say no to friends and relatives who ask for money.

- Comparison shop—you'll save money on your purchases *and* reduce impulse buys.

- Take advantage of free services and activities offered by local libraries and parks.

- Trade in your health-club membership and join the local YMCA or YMHA. These organizations also offer low-cost programs and activities, many geared toward seniors.

- Stay accountable: You and your spouse can encourage each other to keep spending habits in check. If you're single, find another senior friend who'd like a money-buddy and meet at least once a month to share spending victories and struggles.

- Review your insurance coverage (see Chapter 8). When you retire, dropping or reducing life and disability insurance can make sense. Don't buy insurance (or a warranty extension) for anything you can afford to replace.

- If you need a car, consider buying used instead of new, especially if it's certified and still has some warranty protection.

- Always shop with a list to reduce unnecessary purchases.

FIRST PERSON   SUCCESS STORY

Time Is Money

I admit it. I retired without having enough money to keep up my lifestyle. Because I could no longer afford to shop till I dropped, my cleaning lady had to go and I started doing the housework myself. I got pretty fast at it, and the house looked better than it had in years. Still short of money, I decided to quit buying takeout. I dragged out my old cookbooks and began to enjoy fixing my meals, like when I was young. I was soon giving friends treats from my kitchen in lieu of gifts, and inviting people over for lunch instead of meeting them at restaurants. For family birthdays, I gave IOUs promising to chase down comparative prices, or baby-sit, or mend or repair things, or do other time-consuming chores and errands. Instead of giving money to charities, I started volunteering, and met a number of interesting people. Now my money goes a lot further, I'm never bored, and I've got a bunch of new pals, too.

—Tina P., Louisville, Kentucky

financial *planners*

Get professional money help

WHEN YOU HAVE TO MAKE an important health decision, you enlist a doctor. If you need legal help, you call a lawyer. So when it comes to making big money decisions, don't be afraid to contact a certified **financial planner**.

What exactly will a financial planner do for you? If it's your first visit, the planner may ask what prompted your visit. If you want to address an emergency (debt consolidation or handling your company stock options), the planner will help you with that problem. If you ask for a complete fiscal examination, the planner may ask to see your tax returns, investment statements, and other financial documents to help get an overview of your situation. The planner should ask about your goals. Then the planner will recommend some of the best ways to get you where you want to go. This might mean helping you with a budget, or suggesting changes in your investment scheme, or helping you calculate the amount of insurance you need.

FEE ARRANGEMENTS

HOURLY You pay the planner for time spent meeting with you and researching your situation. This is the best place to start if you don't know exactly what you want. Fees range from $75 to $200 per hour.

PERCENTAGE OF ASSETS If you hire an investment adviser to manage your money, the annual fee is usually a percentage of the dollar value of assets managed (usually .75 percent to 1.25 percent). This is the best option if you have $100,000 or more and want ongoing help.

COMMISSION Most brokerage houses and insurance companies offer free retirement planning services to their customers. If you then use a stockbroker or life insurance agent to purchase retirement assets, you pay a commission on anything you buy.

Ⓐsk the experts

Where can I find help in locating a financial planner?

The Garrett Planning Network is a national group of financial advisers committed to providing independent, objective financial advice to average consumers. All of their advisers work on a fee-only basis and charge anywhere from $100 to $200 per hour. Contact them at 866-260-8400 or visit **www.garrettplanningnetwork.com**.

The National Association of Personal Financial Advisors is a national organization with strict membership requirements for admittance. They provide referrals to fee-only planners; call 888-FEE-ONLY or visit their Web site at **www.napfa.org**.

The Financial Planning Association is a national organization of planners. Their Consumer Service and Planner Search (800-282-PLAN or **www.fpanet.org/plannersearch/index.cfm**) provides information about choosing planners and allows you to select planners by ZIP code.

WHO CAN HELP

The following professionals have passed a licensing exam (or series of tests) in their specialty. They must also complete continuing education to keep their license:

Name (Abbreviation)	Area(s) of Expertise
Certified Financial Planner (CFP)	A wide range of financial areas, including taxes, investments, and insurance.
Certified Public Accountant (CPA)	Taxes and accounting.
Certified Financial Analyst (CFA)	In-depth knowledge of investments.
Chartered Life Underwriter (CLU)	Life insurance.

now what do I do?

Answers to common questions

I've tried to budget in the past, but I get overwhelmed pretty easily when I try to figure out what I spend. Any tips?

Start small. Tracking your expenses can indeed be overwhelming. But don't panic. You're not going to be able to track and project every single cup of coffee you buy or newspaper you purchase. But don't let that keep you from trying. First, start collecting receipts from every purchase you make. While you might have to work up the courage to sort through them, you'll need these receipts in order to remember what you've spent. (Some folks prefer to keep a little notebook and then write down everything as they go.) And as you write checks, make sure to write down the date, check number, payee, amount, and description of each. Then once or twice a month, sit down with your receipts and your check register and credit card statements to track what you've spent. If you're PC literate, consider compiling these in personal finance software (like Quicken). If you want to do it by hand, create a blank form like the one on page 11, and make several photocopies. As you pull together the amount you spent in each category for the week, month, or whatever period you decide to track, put the numbers in the appropriate column. Within four to six months you'll probably have enough history to come up with an estimate of what you spend in a year!

My home is full of furniture and crafts I've gathered over the years. Now I want to move to a smaller home. Is there any way to get some extra money for this accumulation of stuff?

First, drop by several antique stores in the neighborhood and talk to the buyers about the items you want to sell. If they think your furnishings sound promising, they may come by and give you an evaluation. (Furniture from the 1950s and 1960s is highly valued by knowledgeable buyers at present.) For items that don't make it as prized heirlooms, consider a yard sale—but only if you have an enterprising spirit, for yard-sale aficionados love to bargain. If you can't haggle with the best of them, put your goods in the hands of a company that runs estate sales, and they will auction your items for you. They'll charge a fee based on a percentage of the sales, but they will take all the hassle out of the experience for you.

OW WHERE DO I GO?!

WEB ADDRESSES

www.quicken.com/retirement/
www.smartmoney.com/retirement/
These sites provide a variety of financial information about retirement planning.

www.seniors.gov
This government site links you to abundant retirement resources.

www.investoreducation.org
This Web site provides a wide variety of resources, including investing basics, help choosing an adviser, and basic information about online investing.

www.invest-faq.com
This site features a collection of frequently asked questions about investments and personal finance, including stocks, bonds, discount brokers, information sources, retirement plans, etc.

www.aaii.com
This American Association of Individual Investors site has information on stocks, bonds, and portfolio management.

www.ftc.gov
The Federal Trade Commission's site provides texts of consumer publications for consumer credit, investments, and telemarketing.

www.pueblo.gsa.gov
This government site provides a wide variety of helpful consumer publications.

PUBLICATIONS

Last Minute Retirement Planning
By Stephen M. Rosenberg, CFP

You've Earned It, Don't Lose It
By Suze Orman

Ernst & Young's Retirement Planning Guide

getting out of *debt*

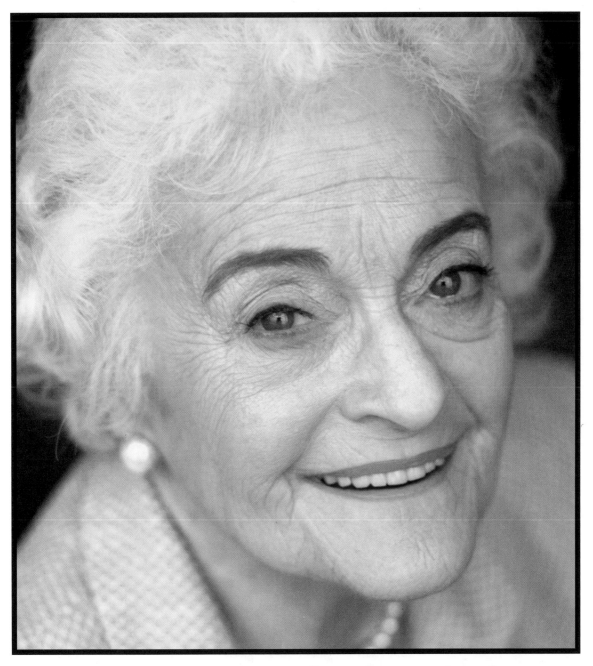

“ *My spouse passed away several years ago, and I'm having trouble living on a fixed income. How can I lower some of my bills?* ”

credit card *debt*

*Avoid high
interest debt*

IF YOU ARE LIKE MANY PEOPLE, when you see something you like in a store, you plunk down your credit card and take it home. Then you pay what you can and let the debt pile up. When you were working, it wasn't so bad—chances are, you even paid a few bills outright. But now that you're retiring, paying ever-mounting credit card bills on a fixed income can quickly become hazardous to your financial health.

What's the problem here? It's called **interest**. As you know, whenever you borrow money, you need to pay for the cost of borrowing it. Why? Because if lenders weren't lending it to you, they could be investing it and earning interest on the investment. You are now their investment, so you have to pay them interest. Banks charge the **prime interest rate** for lending money to their most credit-worthy customers, usually 7 percent to 10 percent. When you sign up for a credit card, however, they can charge any interest rate they want, usually from 9 percent to 20 percent. They call this their **annual percentage rate**, or APR.

And then there's one more tiny problem: it's called **compound interest.** This means that interest will be applied not only to your initial purchase but also to any successive interest you owe. In other words, you will pay interest on interest. Say you buy a large-screen television for $1,000 and charge it on a credit card with an APR of 18 percent. If you just pay the minimum balance of, say, $10 for a year and then pay it off, guess how much you really paid for the television? A whopping $1,183. Compound interest is a bit like yeast in that it feeds on itself. That's why you don't want to carry credit card debt.

ASK THE EXPERTS

How can I find a cheaper credit card?

Online financial Web sites make it easy to find competitive interest rates. Two sites that compile a comprehensive range of card deals are **www.bankrate.com** and **www.bestrate.com**.

How can I switch my balance to a cheaper card?

After finding the best deal, first tell your current card-holder about it and ask them to match it. Often they will, because they don't want to lose your business. If not, inform the company you are switching to, and they'll explain how to transfer the balance.

What happens if I can't make my minimum payment?

Not a good idea. As far as the credit card company is concerned, that minimum payment is a loan payment. If you miss the deadline, they report it to the various credit bureaus that keep track of your credit rating, and it is recorded on your credit report as a missed payment. This can hurt your credit rating.

60 SECOND SAVINGS

If you make purchases just after the monthly closing date for your credit card, you can get a free loan for almost two months. The closing date is the last day that your purchases were recorded for that month's bill. It is usually printed on the bill near the credit and cash advance limits and current balance.

For example: Your card's closing date is August 24, and on August 25 you buy your girlfriend a $150 necklace and earring set for her birthday. When your next bill is issued on about September 3, the charges made after August 24 won't appear on it, so the jewelry charge won't be there. You don't owe anything until the following bill is mailed on October 3. Then you would ideally pay the entire balance by the end of your grace period (usually after 25 days or so).

Compare that with what happens if you pay a small amount every month for a whole year. At the typical credit card interest rate of 17 percent, you pay $175 for the same jewelry.

kicking the credit card *habit*

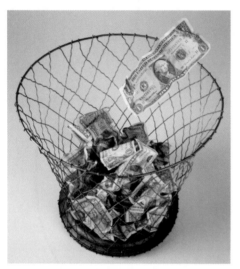

Avoiding the perils of living on credit

LIVING ON A FIXED INCOME can be a shock to many new retirees, especially if their monthly income is lower than what they are used to having. Using credit cards to bridge the gap becomes all too tempting, especially when new credit card offers keep arriving in the mail. Within a year, many new retirees are looking at whopping credit card bills with interest as high as 20 percent. They can't afford to pay it off and they can't afford not to!

Help is at hand. You can extricate yourself from your debt mess. The first thing to do is quit denying that you have a credit problem.

WHAT IF I CAN'T CHANGE BY MYSELF?

If you have trouble breaking the bad-debt syndrome, consider joining Debtors Anonymous, a national not-for-profit collective where you'll find others working to beat the same problem. There are no dues or fees.
P.O. Box 920888
Needham, MA 02492
Tel: 781-453-2743
www.debtorsanonymous.org
E-mail: **new@
debtorsanonymous.org**

STEP BY STEP:

CUTTING BACK

1. SHIFT YOUR DEBTS TO THE LOWEST-INTEREST CREDIT CARD YOU CAN FIND. You can put debt from other cards onto a new card. This makes sense if you get a low-interest-rate card.

2. LIMIT YOURSELF TO ONE CARD. You don't need more than that. Avoid store cards; they're usually the worst deals of all. The 10 percent to 20 percent discount some offer you to sign up is quickly canceled out by the higher interest rates you pay on your purchases.

3. CANCEL ALL OTHER CARDS. You don't want to leave unused credit cards open. Avoid the temptation: Snip the cards and send the issuer a letter informing them you are canceling.

4. THINK OF CREDIT CARDS AS EMERGENCY CASH. Cards can be invaluable in covering a health emergency or necessary car repair. They should be used as backup when your ordinary budget plans go awry— not as mad money that stretches your buying power.

5. DRAW UP A SPENDING BUDGET. Making your expenses fit preset limits is a very effective way to keep debt, especially credit card debt, in check.

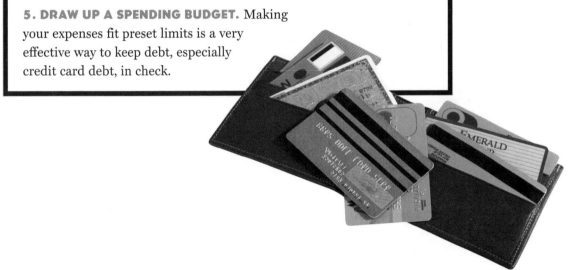

debt *solutions*

You don't have to find a way out all by yourself

IF YOU HAVE HAD TROUBLE with high debt, whatever you do, don't go to one of those "debt doctors" who advertise on a telephone pole or on late-night TV. Private companies often charge high fees, and the field is full of charlatans who prey on desperate people. Also avoid private bill-paying services, especially those that claim they can fix up a poor credit record.

There is, however, reasonable, low-cost help to be had. A credit counselor working for a public or not-for-profit agency is the best way to go. For a small fee, the agency typically contacts all of your creditors, negotiates a moratorium on payments to them, and sets up a plan to repay them. But bear in mind that you will be put on a tight leash until it's over; these payments will be made on a fairly aggressive schedule. Your creditors get much of your incoming cash, while you are allowed to keep only an allowance for your essential living expenses.

If this seems frightening, ask the counselor for help in drawing up a budget. If the budget looks totally impossible, he or she can arrange a more lenient payment schedule.

ASK THE EXPERTS

Can debt consolidators really fix my bad credit rating?

The answer is no. They may claim they can magically clean up a bad credit report, but that is not true. Only you can clean it up, and it's not by using magic. You have to contact each creditor and work out a payment plan. Some may agree to lower your interest rate for this purpose. Once your debts have been paid, you can ask your creditors to report your clean slate to the credit bureaus so your credit history shows your improved status.

How long will it take me to get out of debt?

The answer is usually the same amount of time you have been in debt. In other words, if you have been struggling with too much debt for three years, that's about how long it will take to get clear of it.

Where can I find a credit counselor?

The National Foundation for Consumer Credit is the nation's biggest group of not-for-profit credit counselors. They can direct you to a local office. Consumer Credit Counseling Services, Tel: 800-547-5005.

FIRST PERSON   DISASTER STORY

Over My Head

My husband had his own business and made a good living, but wasn't a great saver. When he died at age 60, there was no retirement nest egg, just some stock that I went through pretty quickly to pay the bills. Social Security didn't come close to what he made. I guess I didn't want to see this, so I just charged things as usual. Before I knew it, I was $30,000 in debt. I got so upset I landed in the hospital with high blood pressure. My kids found out about the debts and paid them, and that made my blood pressure really soar! I had to do something. I got rid of all my credit cards and am learning to live a new way: cash and carry. It was tough at first, but I'm managing. Instead of giving the kids and grandkids things, I give them my time—funny thing, they like that better.

—Miriam S., New York, New York

scams
aimed at
seniors

*How can
you outsmart
them?*

YOU'VE MADE IT THIS FAR without falling prey to swindlers' tricks. Why should you worry now? No matter how sophisticated and educated newly retired folks are, they're prime targets for smooth-talking con artists. An experienced crook knows just how to play on financial fear and insecurity.

While you don't want to become paranoid, it's important to look at how you make decisions. Big-ticket items like vacation homes, insurance, and investments require careful thought, analysis, and discussion—not sales pressure. Even if someone approaches you with a deal that sounds interesting and legitimate, never buy on the first meeting. Instead, gather printed information and say that you'll call back when you have had a chance to look it over. Then analyze the offer.

Let's say someone gives you an intriguing sales pitch for a surefire investment. Ask yourself:

● Do you know anything about the investment? Are they using a lot of technical language to sway you with their expertise? Does the salesman immediately begin pressuring you to sign something? Do you personally know any of the salesperson's clients?

● Are the terms too good to be true, for example, a guaranteed 20 percent return on your investment in the first year? Don't let your need for money blind you to deals that are full of smoke.

● If you decide to go along with the investment, is there any waiting period within which you can back out of the deal? If you change your mind, can you get your money back in full? If the answer is yes, can you get that in writing?

SIGNS OF A SCAM

- **ANYTHING FREE:** TV sets, dinners, or vacations. Remember the old saying: "There's no such thing as a free lunch." If it's free now, you'll no doubt pay for it down the road.
- **A SQUEEZE TO SIGN.** If it's "now or never" and you don't have the option to review the papers with your spouse or adviser before you sign, it's probably a scam.
- **TOO GOOD TO BE TRUE.** If it sounds like that, it probably is—especially "ground floor opportunities" from anyone other than intimate friends or family members. Even loved ones can draw you into an ill-advised investment without meaning to.
- **RECOVERY ROOMS.** Services that help you recover money you've lost from past scams—for a fee—are usually also scams.
- **"CHURNING" FOR FEES.** If a broker frequently suggests buying and selling securities, you might be paying unnecessary commissions.
- **DOOR-TO-DOOR CALLERS.** Few legitimate outfits sell door-to-door these days, and building inspectors, home contractors, and other "professionals" who show up unannounced are rarely on the up-and-up.
- **GET RICH QUICK.** Most newspaper, TV, or radio ads that "guarantee" your ability to get rich quick are really veiled attempts at getting your money from you more quickly.
- **MIRACLE CURES.** Direct mail or other pitches that sell cures for aches, pains, and diseases are rarely aboveboard. Stick with your doctor for medical advice.
- **YOU'RE A BIG WINNER.** Letters claiming you only have to return the card to be a big winner are selling something. Read the fine print and see what you're buying—book, magazine, or something else—and make sure you want it. Your chances of winning a prize are less than they would be in the lottery.

CONSUMER WATCHDOGS

Securities and Exchange Commission (SEC)
Protects consumers from investment fraud. Contact them at 800-SEC-0330 with questions or complaints about investment offerings or investment advisers. They also provide free publications, like "Questions You Should Ask About Your Investments."

Federal Trade Commission (FTC)
Polices everything from fair credit to telemarketers to food labeling to identity theft. Contact their Consumer Response Center (877-FTC-HELP; 202-326-3128; or at **www.ftc.gov**) with complaints or to request free consumer education pamphlets.

Better Business Bureaus
These agencies help consumers fight unfair or deceptive business practices in your area. Check your local phone book for contact information.

now what do I do?

Answers to common questions

If my credit card debt is so bad, how come companies keep offering me more credit cards?

Credit card companies have more liberal lending guidelines than banks or other credit institutions. Credit card companies calculate that you can carry debt equal to 36 percent of your annual gross income, while debt counselors suggest 20 percent. Credit card companies want you to run up bills because they make their profits from all that interest you're paying. So the more you spend, the more often your mailbox seems to fill up with offers for yet more credit cards from companies eager to take advantage of your penchant for spending.

Which debt should I pay first?

Pay down the most expensive debts first—those with the biggest balances at the highest interest rates, since they're costing you the most. Work your way down to the smallest, lowest-interest debts.

What if a creditor is harassing me?

That is against the law. Bill collectors are not allowed to use threats, advertise your debt to the public, or phone you repeatedly about it. If one does, contact the Federal Trade Commission (FTC). It monitors and investigates complaints about consumer credit practices.

Federal Trade Commission
600 Pennsylvania Ave., NW
Washington, DC 20580
Tel: 877-382-4357
www.consumer.gov or **www.ftc.gov**

I have a huge credit card debt at 19 percent. What can I do?

Review all your retirement savings accounts. Use some of that money to pay off your high-interest debt. Then see if you can raise cash by selling or borrowing against any assets, such as a house or car. If you own your home, you can apply for an equity loan using your house as collateral (an asset of yours that the bank can make claim to if you default on the loan). You may also want to consider getting a **reverse mortgage** to help pay down the debt (see page 46). You can also apply for a **personal** or **consolidation loan**. Here a bank agrees to lend you a lump sum of money which you use to pay off your credit card debt. Then you immediately begin paying back the loan, but at a much lower interest rate. If you have no assets, you may need someone who does to co-sign the loan for you.

 **N**OW WHERE DO I GO?!

WEB ADDRESSES	PUBLICATIONS
www.loanweb.com www.bankrate.com	**The Money Diet** by Ginger Applegate
	Guide to Understanding Personal Finance by Kenneth Morris and Alan Siegel
	Your Money or Your Life by Joe Dominguez and Vicki Robin

where do you want to *retire?*

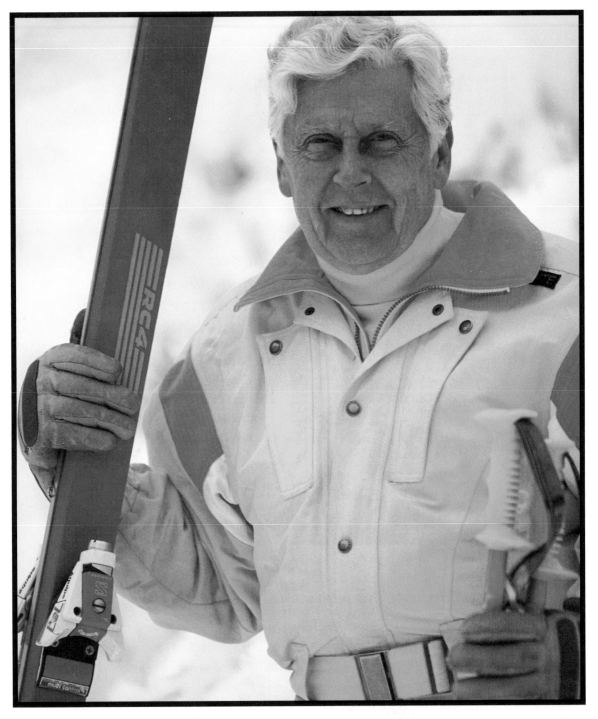

" *I'm itching to move to another part of the country. How can I be sure it will work out before I make the leap?* "

first you *fantasize*

Chances are, you'll live in more than one place during retirement

DECIDING WHERE TO LIVE when you retire can be a bit overwhelming. But don't get discouraged. There are lots of resources to get you started. Here's what you need to consider:

YOUR LIFESTYLE: What do you want to do during your retirement? Baby-sit for the grandkids? Improve your golf handicap? Train for the marathon? Grow tomatoes? Raise money for your favorite charities? Take up scuba diving? Travel as much as possible? Is where you are living now conducive to your retired lifestyle? Or will the weather or location hamper your plans?

YOUR FINANCES: After you retire, how much money will you need to stay where you are? (See page 44.) Can you afford to stay? If you are just getting by, do you want to rent out a room to help defray the cost? Or is it smarter for you to sell and move to a rental?

YOUR HEALTH: This is tricky, but try to imagine your well-being in the next 5 or 10 years. For instance, if you have a bum knee now, it's likely that climbing stairs will prove increasingly difficult in the years to come. In that case, selling your two-story house sooner rather than later might be a good idea.

FACTS TO CONSIDER

Do you have a fantasy about where you want to retire? Maybe you want a tropical beach, or a handy golf course, or a water view. Or you might want to live in another country altogether. Once you identify your dream location, look at how it might measure up in the long run:

- Would your everyday lifestyle fit in your dream location?
- Is the place close enough to friends and family (or far enough away, if you want to keep them at a distance)?
- How's the climate? Is the terrain easy to navigate? Do you notice a lot of seniors walking around?
- Is public transportation accessible? You might reach a point when you or your spouse can no longer drive.
- How available is quality health care?
- Is it easy to do weekly grocery shopping and run errands? If you like restaurants and nice shops, are there some nearby?
- Is the neighborhood a low-crime area?
- How available are events and activities you like: concerts, plays, sports events, museum or library visits, educational opportunities, etc.?
- Are there any activities or services designed just for seniors?
- What about the cost of living and the taxes?

EVALUATING LOCATIONS

Retirement Places Rated: The Single Best Source for Planning the Retirement You Deserve by David Savageau provides an in-depth discussion of many variables for retirement living, and uses them to evaluate 187 cities across the country. The top 10 in the fifth edition are:

1. Fort Collins/Loveland, Colorado
2. Charleston Sea Islands, South Carolina
3. Henderson/Boulder City, Nevada
4. Wickenburg, Arizona
5. St. George/Zion, Utah
6. Boca Raton, Florida
7. Scottsdale, Arizona
8. Tucson, Arizona
9. Prescott/Prescott Valley, Arizona
10. Fort Myers/Cape Coral, Florida

keeping your existing *home*

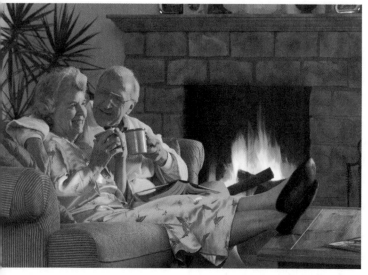

*There's
no place
like it*

MANY PEOPLE WANT TO
remain in the comfortable familiarity of
their own home when they retire. They
enjoy living near family and friends, being
part of their community, and staying in the
place they've called home for many years.
Before you decide to stay put, evaluate
some options:

YOUR LIFESTYLE: Will staying suit your
lifestyle? If your retirement vision is a daily
nature hike, but your home is in the middle
of a big city, you might want to seek out
other possible living arrangements.

YOUR FINANCES: Can you afford to stay put? If your mortgage payment has traditionally consumed most of your paycheck, how will you
cover the monthly expenses with your retirement income? It might be
wise to try to pay off the mortgage before retiring; check with your
financial adviser to find out whether or not selling investments to do
that would be advantageous in your particular situation. If your mortgage is paid off, your adviser may suggest getting a **reverse mortgage**
(see page 46) to give you some money to live on.

YOUR HEALTH: How will your changing physical needs impact where
you live? If you drive everywhere now, you might find your location burdensome if and when you can no longer use your car—unless there's
good public transportation nearby.

Ⓐsk THE EXPERTS

We've always wanted to stay in our home, but now the kids are all married. We're wondering if our house is too big for us. What should we do?

Don't just hang on to your home out of inertia; you're likely to become overwhelmed and let it fall into disrepair. When the house isn't a family hub anymore, and you're ready to spend time on other things, it's time to think about moving on.

I'm itching to move to another part of the country. How can I be sure it'll work out before I make the leap?

Take a test drive before you make a commitment and sell your home. There are several organizations available to help you swap your home with people in other parts of the country. They can help you arrange for a short-term or long-term house swap. Contact HomeLink U.S.A. at 800-638-3841; **www.homelink.org** or HomeExchange at 805-898-9660; **www.homeexchange.com**.

I'm in serious debt. How can I tap the equity in my house?

If you're moving to a smaller home, you can pay off debt with some of the profits from the sale of your old house. If you're staying put, you can apply for a home equity loan or a second mortgage. If you are spending your savings to pay off the debt, a reverse mortgage (page 46) might replace income lost from those savings.

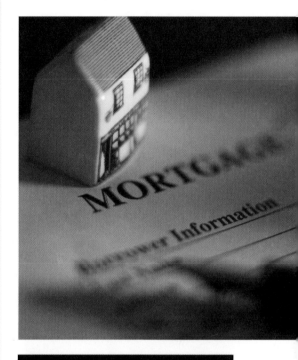

PAYING OFF THE MORTGAGE

Many people find that paying off their mortgage by the time they retire is advantageous, both financially and psychologically. But it isn't always a good idea to tap assets to pay off your debt. It comes down to crunching the numbers. Compare the interest rate your investment earns with the interest rate your loan charges. Which is higher? In most cases, it makes sense to take cash from an asset that earns a low rate of interest to pay a debt with a high rate of interest. But assets earning a high rate of interest usually shouldn't be spent to pay a debt with low interest.

reverse
mortgages

Get money to stay put

IF YOU WANT TO STAY where you are, but you aren't sure you can afford it, a **reverse mortgage** might be your ticket to homestead bliss. You're a good candidate if your house is mostly paid for, you're at least 62 years old, you've maintained your home in good condition, and you plan to live there indefinitely.

In a reverse mortgage, you "sell" the bank your house, but you get to live there for as long as you live. In return, the bank makes a payment (or series of payments) to you, usually for 60 percent of your home's appraised value. Unlike other loans that you need to repay right away, a reverse mortgage isn't repaid until after your house is actually sold, which typically doesn't happen until it's sold by your heirs. (If the heirs want to keep it, they'd have to repay the loan.)

There are three basic types of reverse mortgages:

TENURE REVERSE MORTGAGE—You receive fixed monthly payments for the rest of your life.

TERM REVERSE MORTGAGE—You receive monthly payments for a fixed number of years. The payments are usually higher than those for tenure types.

LINE OF CREDIT REVERSE MORTGAGE—You receive a specified line of credit that you may draw on. Only the amount you use, plus interest, is deducted from the eventual sale price of the house.

You can also get a combination of these methods, or even a lump-sum amount up front. But if you want a lump sum, compare terms of any reverse mortgage offer with regular mortgages, since regular mortgages are often cheaper.

Before you're approved for a reverse mortgage, for your protection, you're required to talk with an independent government-certified credit counselor (no charge). If you have questions about the application procedure, contact HUD (Housing and Urban Development) at 800-569-4287 for a referral, or visit **www.hudhcc.org**. The AARP's Home Equity Information Center (202-434-6042; **www.aarp.org**) can also help.

ASK THE EXPERTS

How much money can I get from a reverse mortgage?

This varies depending on your age, the lender you use, your home's value, the loan costs and interest rates, and the type of loan you choose. If you own your home free and clear, you should get about 60 percent of its worth.

Will a reverse mortgage impact my Social Security benefits?

No—the money you get from the bank is technically a loan, so it does not impact your taxable income, and therefore it will not affect your Social Security. (Remember, it's the amount of money you declare as income on your taxes that impacts your Social Security payment.) However, the proceeds may impact your participation in income-based programs such as Medicaid or food stamps.

How do I shop for a reverse mortgage?

You want to do an apples-to-apples comparison, since the costs associated with a reverse mortgage can vary widely, and may be very high (possibly up to 10 percent of the loan value). Ask each potential lender to give you a **standard cost disclosure**, also known as a total annual loan cost, or TALC. This is a standardized form that banks will give out about their loans to help consumers compare reverse mortgages. Typical costs that show up on this statement include closing costs, insurance, an origination fee, and a monthly servicing fee.

SAMPLES OF REVERSE MORTGAGE MONTHLY PAYMENTS
Based on a home worth $225,000, and an 8 percent interest rate

Your Age	Mortgage Sum	10 Years of Term Payments	Lifetime of Tenure payments
68	$ 85,295	$1,050	$ 642
75	106,899	1,316	854
85	141,108	1,737	1,379

selling your *home*

Make a fresh start

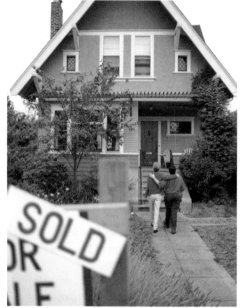

WHAT IF YOU WANT TO SELL? Though moving can be stressful, a fresh start may be just the right thing. If your home is too much to care for, or if keeping it would stretch your budget too far out of line, or if you're looking for a change of venue, leaving for greener pastures can be the answer.

Financially speaking, you could be looking at quite a windfall. Let's say your $300,000 house is fully paid for, but living there would cost $300 a month in property taxes, plus maintenance and cleaning costs of another $200 a month. Then assume that you sell it and invest the proceeds of $280,000 (after closing costs) at, say, 6 percent. You would get $1,400 a month; plus the $500 you'd save by not having to pay property taxes and the ongoing maintenance costs. If you think you could find and enjoy a home or apartment that would cost considerably less than this, then selling your house might be a very sound idea.

Letting go of your house can be a big relief. It might be nice living in a more compact home in a location that is better suited to retirement (think no stairs, easy upkeep, nearby public transportation, sunny climate, etc.).

O.K., there is, of course, the chore of moving, especially if you have to sift through stuff you've accumulated over the years. But look at it this way: You can dispose of your keepsakes exactly as you want. If you stay put and suffer some health setbacks, all that sorting out will be left to your children or other family members. If you do the job now, you could save them the trouble later on.

ASK THE EXPERTS

Unloading our empty nest sounds like a good idea. But where would we go?

You have many options. If you simply want a smaller place, consider checking out condominiums, especially those catering to seniors. Or maybe take the leap and move to another part of the country (see page 52). If you're tired of home ownership, try renting. Look into retirement communities. It's true, some are very expensive, but others are reasonable. Senior living facilities have good security, safety devices, activities, cleaning services, and often meals and other amenities. Start looking early—many of the best ones have waiting lists.

I'm recently widowed. I'd like to stay at home, but I don't want to live alone. Any suggestions?

Finding a roommate can help, whether you're looking for companionship or simply want to reduce your expenses. The National Shared Housing Resource Center (770-395-2625, **www.nationalsharedhousing.org**) coordinates over 300 homesharing programs across the country. They can help whether you're looking to rent a room from someone else, or would like to open up your home to another individual. They also provide careful screening and background checks.

TAX CONSEQUENCES OF SELLING A HOME

The current tax law says that you can sell a home without paying the usual capital gains tax on the first $500,000 in profit ($250,000 if you are single). You must have lived in the house for at least two of the past five years before the sale.

moving far *afield*

Looking for something out of the ordinary?

AS THE POPULATION CONTINUES TO AGE, new retirees are finding or creating living arrangements to fit their lifestyles. Here are some more options that might strike your fancy:

RESORT COMMUNITIES These luxurious retirement communities provide the amenities of resort living: golf, tennis, swimming pool, beaches, marinas, scenic views, exercise rooms, and a variety of dining facilities.

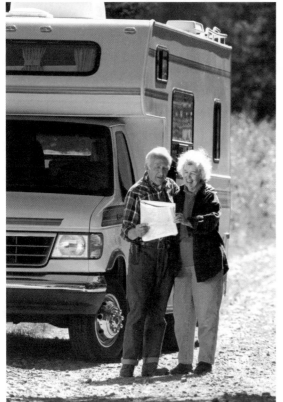

Most have resort prices to match. Call 630-665-8360 or see **www.retirementresorts.com** for more information.

FOREIGN COUNTRIES Some folks long to live out their fantasy of retiring to some tropical island paradise. It's important to investigate how living abroad affects Social Security, voting, visas, income taxes, etc. For example, retirees living abroad aren't eligible for Medicare. Check with American Citizens Abroad (1051 N. George Mason Drive, Arlington, Virginia 22205; fax: 703-527-3269; **www.aca.ch**) or Transitions Abroad (800-293-0373; **www.transitionsabroad.com**) for more information.

RV LIVING Why not go mobile? Some folks can't wait to sell everything they have, buy a motor home, and take that tour of the country they've always dreamed about. See **www.rvamerica.com** or call 480-784-4771 for more information.

ASK THE EXPERTS

I'm thinking about renting a little rustic villa near the Gulf of Mexico for a year to try it out while I rent out my house in Connecticut. What do I need to consider?

It's a great idea to live in your potential retirement location for a test period. It's important, though, to understand the tax consequences before you start. During the time that you rent out your place, you'll have to file a Schedule E with your tax return to report any income you earn from the rental. Of course, you'll get to deduct any related expenses, like advertising, repairs and maintenance, insurance, and any costs of managing the property from afar. You might also be able to deduct any return trips you make to Connecticut during the year, if you can show that the reason for the trip was to manage your rental property. If you decide to move permanently, you'll be able to sell your house with little or no tax consequences as long as you meet the IRS requirements (see pages 48–49). If you continue renting out your home indefinitely, plan on paying tax on the gain.

I'm intrigued by the concept of shared housing, but I'm concerned about living with a stranger. Any tips?

The best shared living arrangements happen when the people involved understand their individual needs and desires and can communicate them to each other. Consider your motivation for the arrangement. Are you simply looking to trim costs? Or do you just want another person in the house to check on you in case you fall or get sick? Or are you looking for a potential companion with whom you can go shopping, take walks, and attend the theater? As long as you and your potential roommate are in sync, sharing a home can be a mutually beneficial experience.

geographical
considerations

Seeking greener (or warmer) pastures

IF YOU'RE SET ON PULLING UP STAKES, where will you go? Maybe a city where you have friends or relatives sounds appealing. Perhaps year-round sunshine and warmth is calling. Maybe you're yearning for a mountain view. Regardless of your motives, it's important to thoroughly check out your prospective surroundings before you actually pick up and go.

How should you start? There are enough "Top 50 Places to Retire" lists to keep you busy investigating for the next few years. But don't let them confuse you. There's really no such thing as the perfect place to retire. After all, everyone's preferences are different—it's a matter of knowing what's important to you. But you can enjoy the process of learning about new cities, investigating your alternatives, and doing your homework.

The process of picking a spot might seem intimidating at first. It's like choosing a marriage partner—sometimes you just know. But like any thoughtful courtship, you need to be patient and get to know your potential mate. Don't rush into anything right away. Consider visiting your possible destination town at least four times (once during each season) before you make a long-term commitment.

BACK TO COLLEGE

College towns are popular choices for seniors because they offer a cross between big city culture and small town friendliness. Many colleges and universities offer lifetime learning opportunities that can help seniors stay active. A good example is the North Carolina Center for Creative Retirement (NCCCR), which is part of the University of North Carolina at Asheville. An integral part of the university, the NCCCR provides local seniors with opportunities for education, leadership, and community service.

WHERE SHOULD I START?

These sources advise on the best places to retire.

Money Magazine
(www.money.cnn.com/retirement)

about.com (seniorhousing.about.com)

Retirement Places Rated, a book by David Savageau containing information about more than 180 cities, along with their weather, crime statistics, activities, medical services, and more.

America's 100 Best Places to Retire, by Richard L. Fox.

FIRST PERSON   SUCCESS STORY

Retiring Right

When I retired, I wanted to just lounge around the house. My wife, Marsha, wanted to move to a retirement community, but I persuaded her that we'd be better off staying in our own place. After all, the mortgage was paid off, and I was still fit, so I could take care of the maintenance. The kids did come over every Sunday for dinner, and Marsha had always liked cooking for them. But soon I realized that although I had retired, she was still doing the same work she had always done—cleaning the house, doing the laundry, running the errands, fixing the meals. I was having fun, but she had no more free time than she'd had before. Then my eyesight began to go, and we finally had to move to a retirement community. It has housekeeping services, two meals served every day, and a van to take us to stores and doctors' appointments. There are lots of activities for us to enjoy here. And now the kids have us over to their house for Sunday dinner. Marsha loves it. I wish we'd moved earlier, so Marsha could have retired when I did.

—**Martin L., Phoenix, Arizona**

senior living *alternatives*

Can you get along on your own, or do you need assistance?

THERE ARE SEVERAL STYLES OF GROUP accommodations, sometimes referred to as "congregate living." Here's an overview of what they include.

INDEPENDENT LIVING Also called retirement communities, these are geared toward seniors who want to remain independent but who may want the convenience of meals, housekeeping, some shared activities, and transportation to shops and doctors if needed. Many communities have a nurse on duty, and may allow people to use electric carts to get around the halls or paths. Often transportation is available to take residents to markets, shops, and doctors, and special outings may be planned as well. If you go this route, you're on your own to pay for it—no insurance or federal assistance will help.

ASSISTED LIVING These units provide the same wide range of services as independent-living facilities, plus personal and medical care for people who are not as robust physically as they once were. Services range from simple medication reminders to help with **activities of daily living** (ADL), such as shopping, bathing, grooming, and dressing, as needed, in addition to many services independent-living facilities might offer. Long-term care insurance (see page 138), and possibly Medicaid (see page 142) may help defray assisted-living costs.

NURSING HOMES These long-term care (or skilled nursing) facilities provide 24-hour support for people with chronic and long-term illnesses, who need more than limited assistance. They generally provide a full range of services, including daily nursing care, and dietary and therapeutic assistance. Medicaid and long-term care insurance can help defray these costs, and Medicare may chip in for short-term stays.

CONTINUING CARE RETIREMENT COMMUNITIES (CCRC) These communities combine all three types of living arrangements mentioned above in adjacent facilities. They allow retirees to graduate as needed from independent-living quarters to assisted-living quarters and then to a nursing home—all in one location (usually a campus setting). Residents "age in place" without having to move every time their situation changes. Such facilities are especially convenient for couples; if one requires nursing care, the other lives close enough to visit easily.

ASK THE EXPERTS

How much does it cost to live in a retirement community with continuing care?

The facilities can be vastly different, and so can the prices. Some communities are made up of a cluster of cottages or a renovated apartment building, while others consist of luxurious houses and town houses grouped in a country-club setting. Although a few continuing-care communities provide rental arrangements, an up-front payment is usually required (anywhere from about $30,000 for a studio apartment to several hundred thousand dollars for a detached home) in addition to ongoing monthly fees. The up-front payment may be nonrefundable or only partially refundable to your heirs when you die. The monthly fees increase as you move from one level of care to the next.

I've heard there's a lot of paperwork involved when you move into a congregate-living facility. Can I get stung?

It's a good idea to have an elder-care attorney, an accountant, or another senior specialist review the contracts and fee structures of all congregate-care facilities before you sign up, to help you evaluate all the costs. The payments and fees for continuing-care residences, assisted-living facilities, nursing homes, Medicare (page 130), medigap insurance, and any long-term care insurance you have (page 140) can all impact your income taxes. Even the initial or monthly fees for a living facility may be considered medical expenses and might be partially deductible. But if you move away, part of any up-front payment you make could be forfeited. Also, if you don't have unlimited funds, you will want to find out if the assisted-living and nursing-care facilities you are considering accept Medicaid, and when and how you might be eligible for it.

evaluating retirement *communities*

A RETIREMENT COMMUNITY IS USUALLY an independent-living facility, often with continuing-care amenities, such as medical assistance or help with activities of daily living. Choose a retirement community very carefully. Before you visit one, call for a brochure and compare the information in it with this checklist. If questions remain unanswered, ask them by phone. Based on what you find out, you will be able to decide which facilities you will actually visit.

Call first, then visit

✔ Do units have private, full bathrooms? Step-in showers?

✔ Do units have cooking capabilities?

✔ Do units have individually controlled heating and cooling?

✔ How extensive are housekeeping services?

✔ What security procedures are in effect in the building?

✔ What types of religious services are available?

✔ Are there guest accommodations?

✔ Is there a beauty/barber shop?

✔ Is there access for the handicapped?

✔ Are there several meal plans? Can special dietary needs be met?

✔ What types of social activities are provided?

- ✔ What types of medical, rehabilitative, and therapeutic services are available?
- ✔ What are the costs and fees?
- ✔ Which services cost extra?
- ✔ If there is a nursing facility, does it accept Medicaid? Medicare?

EVALUATING A RETIREMENT COMMUNITY

When you narrow down your options based on location, costs, and services, make appointments for thorough tours of your top choices. Here are points to cover:

- ✔ Talk to the administrator. Does he or she answer questions readily? Ask to see the facility's license and the administrator's license. Are they up-to-date? Review the facility's inspection reports. Are there any issues or problems noted? If so, have they been resolved?

- ✔ Talk to the staff. Are they pleasant? Patient? Do they seem easily available to residents and guests? Are there enough of them?

- ✔ Is the living unit you are considering convenient to the dining room? Is there ample closet and storage space? Are there emergency call buttons or pull cords in the room? Grab bars in the bathroom? Is there enough privacy?

- ✔ Investigate the medical services. What happens in case of emergencies?

- ✔ Is the lighting bright enough in the common areas? Are there handrails in the hallways? Room for electric carts in the hall? Wheelchair accessibility? Elevators?

- ✔ Are there fire sprinklers? Smoke detectors? How secure are the residents' units? The facility itself?

- ✔ Are the public rooms and activity rooms neat? Attractive? Are the lawns and gardens well kept? If there's a pool, is it clean?

- ✔ Eat a meal. How's the quality and taste of the food? Look at the weekly menus. Is there enough variety? Are the menus nutritious? Are the kitchen and dining areas clean and inviting?

- ✔ Talk to the residents. Ask them what they like about the place. Ask what they don't like. Do their interests seem to be similar to yours?

moving and *taxes*

Cost of living, taxes, and other dollar signs

SOME PEOPLE MOVE TO A DIFFERENT state just to save on income taxes. While saving money is always fun, especially if you are on a fixed income, don't make hasty decisions just because a state doesn't have an income tax. Here's why:

● Low or no state income tax doesn't mean total tax relief. For example, Florida doesn't have a state income tax. They do, however, have an "intangibles tax" that taxes nonretirement plan savings. Since most retirees have high accumulated savings, but not huge incomes, this tax structure can actually be a liability rather than a benefit. You should also consider real-estate taxes, sales taxes, and whether Social Security and pension benefits are taxed. Remember—every state gets money to conduct its business somehow.

● Because your income may be lower during retirement, taxes probably won't be as burdensome as before. When you were in the 27 percent, 30 percent, 35 percent, or 38.6 percent federal income tax bracket, every dollar of deductions counted, and every additional dollar of income got taxed heavily. But many retirees find themselves in the lowest 10 percent federal income tax bracket, so their overall tax burden is more manageable. Even the tax rate in a high income tax state like California is less than 10 percent. When combined with a 15 percent federal income tax, the total percentage is still less than you probably paid during your high-earning years.

● Taxes are just one component of the total cost of living (the price of housing, utilities, food, clothing, etc.), which is the real issue to take into account. Consider Arkansas, for example. The state income tax rate ranges up to a hefty 7 percent, but the overall cost of living is lower than in most other states.

STATE TAXES AT A GLANCE

Add the following information into the mix of ingredients you're considering as you ponder moving. But if you find yourself putting a lot of weight on these factors, make sure to visit your accountant before making any final decisions.

TAX ADVANTAGES

States with no income tax

Alaska
Florida
Nevada
New Hampshire
South Dakota
Tennessee
Texas
Washington
Wyoming

States with no sales tax

Alaska
Delaware
Montana
New Hampshire
Oregon

TAX DISADVANTAGES

States that tax Social Security benefits

Colorado
Connecticut
Iowa
Kansas
Minnesota
Missouri
Montana
Nebraska
New Mexico
North Dakota
Utah
Rhode Island
West Virginia
Vermont
Wisconsin

States with no real-estate tax breaks for seniors

Florida
Louisiana
Minnesota
Oregon
Vermont
Wisconsin

now what do I do?

Answers to common questions

I've found a beautiful retirement community, but I don't know if I will really like living there. How can I make up my mind?

Almost all of these communities have guest rooms with very reasonable rates. Move into one for a week or two and take part in all the activities. If you like the residents and enjoy many of the activities, it's a good bet you will enjoy living there. And the guest-room rent for the week is a small price to pay compared to the cost of moving if you find out later that you don't like it.

What expenses for assisted living or nursing care will be covered by long-term care insurance, Medicare, or Medicaid?

Medicare usually only pays for a short period of care following a hospitalization (see page 130). Depending on your policy, long-term care insurance not only pays a per diem if you go into a nursing home, but it also pays for an aide as soon as you need assistance with two or three activities of daily living (or ADLs). ADLs include eating, dressing, bathing, using the toilet, and transferring in and out of beds and chairs. Assistance with ADLs is not limited to congregate-care facilities; you can get help in your own home as well. You will get similar payments from Medicaid, provided you have no other source of income.

I've heard that refinancing my existing mortgage is a good idea. Should I do it?

If your motivation to refinance is pulling out cash from your home, you may want to compare the costs of refinancing with a reverse mortgage (see page 46). It might also make sense to refinance if you have at least 10 years remaining on your current mortgage and can reduce your rate by at least 1.5 percent to 2 percent—provided you plan on living in the house for many years to come.

I'm feeling a little overwhelmed at the prospect of selling my home that I've lived in for the past 40 years. Who can I turn to for help with the real estate market?

Consider calling a Senior Real Estate Specialist. These specially trained real estate agents have completed certain courses and other prerequisites geared toward helping older individuals find homes that meet their needs. You can locate one at **www.seniorsrealestate.com**, or call 800-500-4564.

OW WHERE DO I GO?!

WEB ADDRESSES

American Association of Homes and Services for the Aging
www.aahsa.org
National nonprofit organization representing 5,600 not-for-profit nursing homes, continuing-care communities, assisted-living residences, and community service organizations for the elderly. (AAHSA, 2519 Connecticut Avenue NW, Washington, DC 20008-1520; Tel: 202-783-2242; Fax: 202-783-2255).

www.50states.com
Provides a variety of information about all 50 states, including fun facts, virtual tours, weather, and real estate (50 States, Box 2216980, Santa Clarita, CA 91322).

www.homemods.org
National Resource Center on Supportive Housing and Home Modification, 3715 McClintock Avenue, Los Angeles, CA 90089-0191; Tel: 213-740-1364; Fax: 213-740-7069.

PUBLICATIONS

Retirement Places Rated
By David Savageau

AARP: *Housing* and *Selecting Retirement Housing* pamphlets
800-424-3410

Money magazine annual issue on "Best Places to Live"

America's Best Places to Retire
By Richard L. Fox

Fifty Fabulous Places to Retire in America
By Kenneth A. Stern and Lee Rosenberg

Home Planning for Your Later Years: New Designs, Living Options, Smart Decisions, How to Finance It
By William K. Wasch

staying *active*

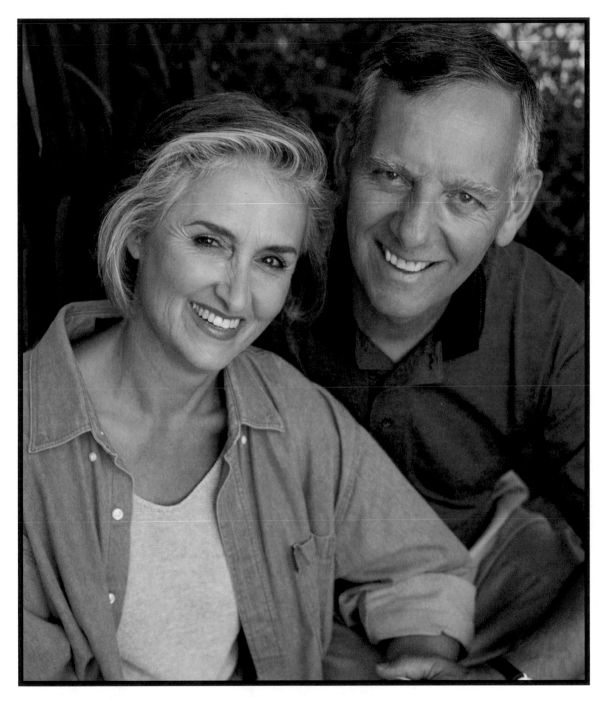

We love to travel. How can we find other retirees who share our travel interests?

indulge your *hobbies* and interests

Time to do what you want

PEOPLE ARE RIGHT IN THINKING that retirement is the time to do all the things they've been putting off—acting in community theater, golfing every day, cooking French food, growing prize roses, painting portraits, or reading Homer's *Odyssey*—in Greek. If you're an avid photographer, for example, you can now pursue your hobby full throttle and enter photography contests, take courses, join clubs, and spend as much time taking pictures as you like.

But what if you spent so much time working that you didn't get a chance to develop many outside interests? Or if you've lost interest in the hobby you thought you'd pursue once you retired? Take heart. A healthy retirement is about change and growth. The trick is to find interests that intrigue you. Here are some considerations for finding a new hobby you'll enjoy:

● **Do you enjoy being alone, or do you prefer a group?** All hobbies have certain events that bring enthusiasts together, but for some hobbies, such as playing bridge, you need a group, whereas other hobbies, such as writing poems, require periods of solitude.

● **Be realistic about your talent, your patience—and your expectations.** If you're just learning to knit, will you get discouraged trying to make that intricately patterned mohair coat? Start with a simple scarf.

● **How much do you need to spend to get started?** It's wise to keep initial costs low until you're sure you really enjoy a particular hobby. Rent—rather than buy—a violin, for instance, during the first few months of lessons.

- **Consider the space limitations in your home.** If you move to smaller living quarters, will you have enough space for a table saw?
- **Talk over your plans with your spouse.** Do you expect him or her to join you on the golf course? How much time do you imagine you'll be spending there? Will your spouse resent your being gone that long?

COMMUNITY GROUPS

If it's a structured activity that you seek, community centers and senior clubs offer many such events for retirees. Membership fees are low (or free), and you can get involved as much, or as little, as you wish. This is an ideal way to make new friends who share common interests. Churches and synagogues run programs, too, that offer lunches, study groups, and bus trips to nearby points of interest. Often the programs are nonsectarian; that is, you may not have to be Catholic to attend a church's bingo night or join their string ensemble. Civic groups run clubs for retirees, as well. The Rotary Club, for example, sponsors Probus clubs for retired men and women who are active volunteers. They sponsor social events and schedule speakers to keep members informed about local issues.

FIRST PERSON   SUCCESS STORY

A Priceless Legacy

After I retired, I had free time to spend with my grandchildren, and I began to tell them stories about my own childhood. They love to hear about the "olden days." One day my daughter, their mom, overheard me telling the kids how we used to shear sheep on the farm. She said she'd never heard it, and asked me to write it down for her, because after me there would be no one who knew about the way things were back then. Soon I started writing a page or two every day—nothing complicated, just how things were different when I was young—the first telephone we had, the first tractor we owned, how my dad fought in World War II. Soon after that I took a course in writing family history at the local community college, and my cousin and I gathered up all the old family pictures we could find and labeled them with names and dates as best we could discover them. I've continued to write about the good old days, and now I've started compiling our genealogy. At all the family gatherings, everyone crowds around to hear what I've found. They all love what I'm doing for the family. I love it, too.

—**Lee F., Billings, Montana**

start a second *career*

Strike out in new directions

MANY RETIREES STAY with the job they know—they are rehired as consultants by their old firm. They can often set their own hours while keeping a more independent stance. That way their situation may be less pressured than their old job was (see opposite page).

Other retirees want to work, even need to work, but not at the same old job. They want to go on to new careers. If you are ready to explore a change but think you're not qualified to do anything but sell software, for example, or balance the books, you may be shortchanging yourself. With a lifetime of experience from your paid employment—and from your volunteer activities, interests, and various home and social roles, too—you may have more skills than you realize. Can you write reports and memos? Supervise others? Gather information? Organize records? Lead a group? While you may have used any or all of those skills at your old job, they are certainly not limited to one particular occupation or profession. Other, completely different jobs may require similar skills.

If you're thinking about changing careers, take some concrete steps:

- Assess your skills by listing them on a piece of paper.
- Network with friends and business associates to get their opinion about how good a fit you'd be in the new field. Ask them for job leads and/or introductions to others in the profession.
- Find out if you'll need formal training for the job you have in mind.
- Consider volunteering in the desired field to gain some experience and to make some connections.

SAME JOB. . .DIFFERENT HOURS

I loved my job, but hated the daily stress and grind. How can I keep my hand in?
Lots of people retire "officially," yet they continue to work in their old professions—but at a reduced level. Some retirees cut back to two or three days per week, for example. Others work just a few hours every day. Such arrangements need to be worked out in advance with your boss and/or the human resources department before you retire. In some cases, your part-time stint can run indefinitely; in other cases, it's for a limited time only. The deal you cut will depend on your employer, your relationship with the company, and the type of work that you do.

A lot of retirees I know consult or work freelance. Some get paid by the project, some by the hour. Which is better?
In the final analysis, it comes down to your time. If you know how many hours are involved in a project, then you can calculate a project fee. If you don't know how a project will pan out, consider charging by the hour to make sure you get paid for any unforeseen "overtime." A note of caution: When you work on a project basis, you're often called in when deadlines are bearing down on regular employees. You may find those deadlines affect you as well. After 12 straight hours at your desk trying to help your colleagues out of a jam, you may well wonder if this is the way you want to spend your retirement.

START YOUR OWN BUSINESS

At some point in our lives, we've all dreamed of owning our own business. But for most of us, it has remained just that: a dream. Being an entrepreneur is risky—and time consuming. (You generally need to pump a lot of money into a fledgling business, too.) Still, running your own business can be rewarding, and lots of retirees have done it successfully.

Do you have what it takes to succeed? Consider the following questions before you take action:

- What kind of business do I want? (Can my hobby become a business?)
- How much money is needed to start the business? How much money will I need to keep it going?
- Am I prepared to work really hard?
- Do I have a business plan?
- How will I get started? What resources do I have?
- Do I have someone I can ask for guidance during the start-up?

check out *volunteer* work

Keep using your experience and skills

YOU WANT AN ACTIVE, meaningful life after retirement without taking a job? Volunteering can fill the bill. Nearly half of all people aged 55 and older volunteer at least one day a year. Many people log far more volunteer days than that, of course—and in a surprising number of occupations. These giving souls work not just as aides in hospitals and schools, but as tutors and foster grandparents, proofreaders and programmers, nature guides, and special-events coordinators.

Volunteering lets you "give back" to a community. For many folks, that can be enormously rewarding. In fact, it can improve your life in a concrete way. Research has proved that regular volunteering prolongs life expectancy and improves physical and psychological well-being. Why? When you volunteer, you tend to feel better about yourself and the world around you. You also may feel less isolated, less absorbed with your own problems and worries.

Doing good, though, isn't the only reason to volunteer. It can give you the opportunity to meet new and interesting people who share your passion for, let's say, saving endangered animals. For many retirees, volunteer work also provides structure and routine—a natural extension of your working life. You can continue to use skills and talents you've developed over the years—but in new and interesting ways.

FINDING VOLUNTEER WORK THAT'S RIGHT FOR YOU

AARP (American Association of Retired Persons) suggests using the following questions as a guide:

1. Why do I want to do volunteer work?

2. What are the benefits I expect to derive from my volunteer service?

3. What particular knowledge, skills, or aptitudes do I have to offer?

4. What are my strengths?

5. What do I like doing? What do I dislike doing?

6. Do I enjoy working alone or with others?

7. Is there something I want to learn how to do?

8. Is there a particular problem or issue that I care about? What really interests me?

9. Would I rather work with people, things, or ideas?

10. Am I willing to travel?

11. How much time am I willing and able to give?

12. Are weekends or weekdays best? What part of the day—morning, afternoon, or evening—would suit me best?

WHAT'S OUT THERE?

- Points of Light Foundation (800-865-8683) connects you with local volunteer opportunities through its national network of volunteer centers.

- Habitat for Humanity International (800-422-4828; **www.habitat.org**) builds homes for needy families, both here and abroad.

- The Special Olympics (800-700-8585; **www.specialolympics.org**) provides sports training and athletic competition for children and adults with mental retardation.

- Marine Toys for Tots Foundation (**www.toysfortots.org**) collects, wraps, and distributes toys for kids during the holiday season.

- The Susan G. Komen Breast Cancer Foundation (800-653-5355; **www.komen.org/race/**) sponsors the Race for the Cure.

- The Virtual Volunteering Project (**www.serviceleader.org/vv**) provides information on more than 100 organizations across the U.S. that use online volunteers to do research, tutor students, and translate languages (among many other jobs).

take a *trip*

*Now's the
time
to get up
and go*

MOST PEOPLE TALK ABOUT TRAVELING as they do about losing those last five pounds: I'll do it someday. Well, guess what? That someday may be here at last. In retirement, you're no longer constrained by work or family commitments. You have the time to travel. Your biggest problem, in fact, may be picking a destination.

If there's a culture you've always wanted to know more about, a cuisine you adore, or a style of architecture you want to study, that's a good starting point for picking the place you want to visit. In which towns, cities, or countries can you pursue those interests?

Next, think about how long you want to stay at a particular destination. Then consider your budget. That may not be as tough as it once was. As a senior, you can take advantage of money-saving senior discounts. For example, join AARP and save up to 25 percent on airfare, hotels, motels, resorts, car rentals, and cruises. (To join, you must be over 50; there's a $10 annual membership fee.)

Finally, decide if you want to travel alone, with a spouse or partner, with friends, or as part of a group. And before you pooh-pooh the group option, keep in mind that times have changed. Senior group travel doesn't necessarily mean a bus trip that shuttles you from one sight to another anymore. (See page 72.) Today, the over-50 crowd demands more challenging adventures, both physically and intellectually. You can take a tour to hike, paint, cook, study, or even learn a language with other like-minded retirees.

VOLUNTEER AND SEE THE WORLD

Commitments vary from a week to a few months. Some volunteer travel programs pay for your travel expenses, but if you pay, they may be tax-deductible.

- Elderhostel Service Programs (877-426-8056; **www.elderhostel.org**) Go to far-off places—some foreign— where you build homes, teach children, catalog artifacts.

- Global Volunteers (800-487-1074; **www.globalvolunteers. org**) Help handicapped children in Ecuador, for example, or teach English in southern Italy.

- Earthwatch Institute (800-776-0188; **www.earthwatch.org**) Work with scientists and conservationists on field research projects in 50 countries.

- The International Executive Service Corps (203-967-6000; **www. iesc.org**) Business and professional types become consultants in developing countries.

- Health Volunteers Overseas (202-296-0928; **www.hvousa. org**) Nurses, physical therapists, doctors, and other health professionals go to work in developing countries.

travel with a *group*

Take a trip with retirees who share your interests

VIEW PINK DOLPHINS. Improve your Spanish. Hike in the Himalayas. Or take an African safari with your grandchild. These aren't your father's "old folks" tours. Rather, they're educational, cultural, historical, and athletic adventures that will inspire and enrich your life. You'll meet new friends, learn new things, and, yes, visit new places. The main advantage of a tour is that most everything—booking, baggage handling, driving, and obtaining tour guides—is done for you.

Typically, you have to be at least 50 years of age to sign up for treks designed for retirees, but if your spouse or traveling partner is younger, he or she will be allowed to go with you. Here's a sampling of what these senior groups have to offer:

ELDERHOSTEL (877-426-8056; **www.elderhostel.org**) provides educational adventures throughout the world. You can pan for gold in the Yukon, for example, or get an insider's view of the Metropolitan Museum. Their catalogs include some 2,000 different educational and cultural trips. Inspired by the youth hostels of Europe, Elderhostel offers low rates: A six-night stay for a U.S. trip, for example, costs about $500 plus round-trip transportation.

SENIOR WORLD TOURS (888-355-1686; **www.seniorworldtours.com**) offers snowmobiling adventures in Yellowstone National Park and in Alaska. Trips run for 6 to 10 days.

GRAND TRAVEL (800-247-7651; **www.grandtrvl.com**) organizes cultural and educational vacations for grandparents—and their grandchildren (ages 7 to 17)—in the U.S., Europe, Africa, and Australia. Groups are limited to 20 people. The most popular trip: the two-week African safari in Kenya.

SENIOR WOMEN'S TRAVEL (212-838-4740; **www.poshnosh.com**) specializes in cultural tours "for women only" to Paris, Venice, London, and more. The group also offers a grandmother/granddaughter trip to Paris.

ELDERTREKS (800-741-7956; **www.eldertreks.com**) offers adventure travel to remote destinations such as Iceland, Transylvania, Tibet, and the Galapagos Islands. Groups are small (just 16 people). All trips involve walking; some also include hiking in the rain forest, for example, or sailing (with a small crew) off the coast of British Columbia.

EUROPEAN WALKING TOURS (217-398-0058; **www.walkingtours.com**) lets you "walk" through Italy, Austria, Switzerland, Spain, or France. No backpacking is involved, though. You're based in a hotel and spend your days exploring the region on foot. The trip to the Dordogne area of France, for instance, lets you explore the prehistoric caves.

WALKING THE WORLD (800-340-9255; **www.walkingtheworld.com**) tours some 27 destinations in the U.S. and around the world. By day you'll walk the countryside; by night, you'll sleep in a bed-and-breakfast or a country inn. Groups are limited to 16.

ODYSSEYS UNLIMITED (888-370-6765; **www.odysseys-unlimited.com**) offers fully escorted cultural and sightseeing tours to China, Spain, and other countries outside North America. Groups are relatively small (no more than 24 people per group).

OVER THE HILL GANG, INTERNATIONAL (719-389-0022; **www.othgi.com**) sets up skiing, rafting, biking, and golfing adventures in the U.S., Canada, Europe, and South America. On one trip, you bike through Holland; on another, you play golf in Ireland.

PHOTO EXPLORER TOURS (800-315-4462; **www.photoexplorertours.com**) focuses on photography. Although this group isn't limited to those over 50, most people who take the tour are retirees. The company, which is run by travel photographer Dennis Cox, now offers up to a dozen programs annually, which include trips to China, Tibet, and Nepal.

MALACA INSTITUTO (011-34-95-229-3242; **www.malacainst-ch.es**) organizes a special two-week vacation program for seniors who want to improve their Spanish. Lessons in "practical" Spanish are combined with cooking lessons, museum visits, dance classes, and more.

go back to *school*

You're never too old to learn

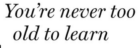

ALTHOUGH YOU MAY BE FAR from "college age," most universities have a lot to offer students who are retired. You can take college courses in any subject that interests you—without having to matriculate toward a degree. Some regular college courses, however, do have prerequisites. That is, to take a more advanced course, such as Understanding Shakespeare and His Times, you may have to take other, more basic, courses first.

If you'd like to earn a degree, you can, of course. There's no age limitation on working toward a college diploma or even an advanced degree. Many retirees, though, are just interested in expanding their horizons—not going for a cap and gown. Your best bet, then, are courses offered through the college's continuing education department. These classes can be taken for credit (but aren't always), have fewer prerequisites, and are geared toward returning students—both young and older—who attend school simply because they want to learn more about ecology, or the Romantic poets, or Aristotle's philosophy.

If money is an issue, check out your local high schools. Many of them offer adult education courses which are generally lower in cost. And some colleges allow you to audit courses for a small fee. As an auditor, you can't participate in the discussions, but you can listen to the exchange, and of course, enjoy the lectures.

If traveling to and from campus is a problem, some universities now offer online courses, complete with chat rooms and teacher conferences. In fact, if you want to take courses from a famous university in another part of the country, online courses may give you the opportunity to do so. For free courses, check the listings on **www.bnuniversity.com**, sponsored by Barnes & Noble. You'll be most successful with online study if you are self-motivated and enjoy learning by reading and writing rather than by listening.

ASK THE EXPERTS

I've heard about these Institutes for Learning in Retirement. What makes their offerings different from other continuing education classes?

For starters, there are absolutely no prerequisites (except for a love of learning); no credit is given; no tests or grades either; and, obviously, these courses won't lead to a degree. What's more, the prices are downright cheap. At some schools, you pay $75 to $100 per term (for as many courses as you want to take during that time period) or about $25 per course. For more information, ask about an Institute for Learning in Retirement (ILR) at your local college or university.

Who teaches ILR classes?

Most institutes rely on volunteer "moderators." Often, these moderators are retired teachers who may be teaching a subject they love—but not one they necessarily taught professionally. At one college, for instance, a retired professor of pharmacology teaches a course in classical music.

GIVE BACK

Want to go back to school—as a teacher? Consider RE-SEED. That's Retirees Enhancing Science Education Through Experiments and Demonstration (617-373-8388; **www.reseed.neu. edu**). This Northeastern University program prepares engineers, scientists, and others with a science background to assist middle-school teachers in teaching physical science one day per week for a year.

now what do I do?

Answers to common questions

My wife and I both love to read. In fact, we have stacks of books that we haven't had time to read. But she says that won't keep us occupied during our retirement. I disagree. Who's right?

In some ways, you both are. While it's great that you both share the same interest, reading is a rather solitary interest that probably won't sustain you day after day. To make it work, you need to "expand" the concept. How about joining or forming a book club with others? Or perhaps you might take a literary trip that tours some of the sites mentioned by an author you both enjoy.

I was looking forward to volunteering in my local elementary school after I retired from my job as a teacher. But after a few months, I found that I resented working as a volunteer for the same tasks that I used to get paid for. Any suggestions?

While some people are happy to volunteer the expertise and skill that they honed on the job, many other retirees feel as you do. Look for a paid position that lets you use your teaching skills, and then volunteer to do work that is unrelated to your former job. You're not likely to have the same problem volunteering to address envelopes or answer phones, for example, for the American Lung Association.

I'm not able to get around easily because of my arthritic knees, but I really like to be with people. Is there any way I can join in senior activities in my community?

Make an appointment with a social worker who specializes in caring for older people. You will be surprised to find that she may have access to transportation services for seniors that could get you to many events, such as concerts and lectures at local universities, activities at community centers, and classes at your local Y.

I've been dying to travel when I retire, but now that we have the time, my wife doesn't want to. She says it's too much trouble to get someone to look after our cats, and she hates packing, and she doesn't like to fly. I'm so disappointed.

Perhaps your wife, seeing how much you'd like to travel, wouldn't mind if you went on trips without her once in a while. You could travel with groups such as Elderhostel (see page 72) if you don't want to be absolutely on your own. But discuss how she would feel being at home alone. She might like to have a friend come to stay with her while you are away.

My husband just started using a wheelchair and is worried we won't be able to travel anymore. How can I convince him otherwise?

There are many organizations to help make traveling a breeze for the disabled. Check these sources for options:

- Access-Able Travel Source (303-232-2979; **www.access-able.com**)
- Global Access Disabled Travel Network (**www.geocities.com/paris/1502**)
- Accessible Vacation Home Exchange (**www.independentliving.org/vacaswap.html**)
- Accessible Journeys (800-846-4537; **www.disabilitytravel.com**)

NOW WHERE DO I GO?!

WEB ADDRESSES

www.aarp.org
Contains information about everything from volunteer programs to life transitions to money and work issues.

www.careerplanner.com
Offers online career planning and career counseling. Includes an online career planning test to assess your interests and capabilities.

www.myseniors.com
Features information on travel, money, shopping, entertainment, lifestyle, and more.

www.Freedom.goGrrl.com
Offers articles on leisure and retirement for boomers and seniors.

PUBLICATIONS

How to Retire Happy
By Stan Hinden

What Do You Want to Do When You Grow Up: Starting the Next Chapter of Your Life
By Dorothy Cantor and Andrea Thompson

101 Secrets for a Great Retirement: Practical, Inspirational, and Fun Ideas for the Best Years of Your Life
By Mary Helen Smith and Shuford Smith

social security

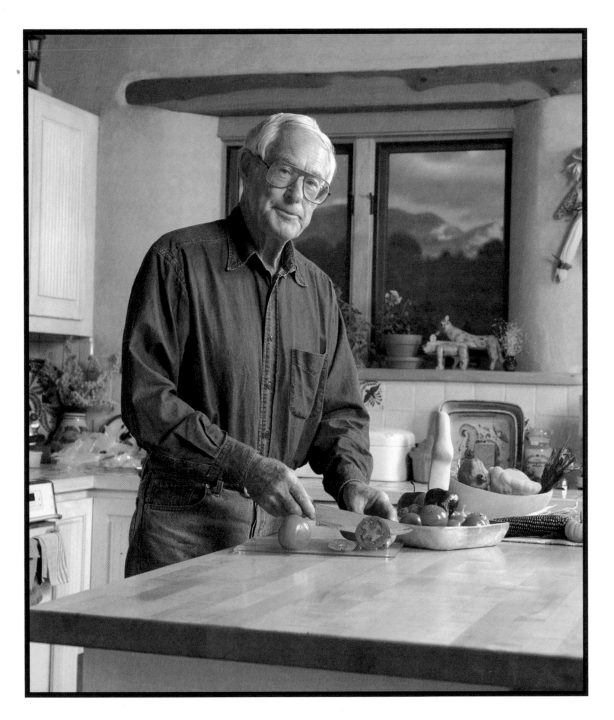

I want to continue working after I retire. Will my salary affect my Social Security payment?

time to start *collecting*

Provide the financial base for your retirement

SOCIAL SECURITY. DID YOU EVER THINK you'd see the day when this was more than just another paycheck deduction? When it would actually start to improve your cash flow? Well, with retirement, the time is here at last.

To be eligible, you or your spouse needs to have accumulated 40 **credits** during your working years. (You earn up to 4 of these credits per year of work, so most people qualify within 10 years of full-time employment.) For most people, their Social Security benefit is calculated using an average of their highest 35 years of earnings. Depending on their ages and when they started collecting, non-working widows and widowers of qualified working spouses can receive between 71 percent and 100 percent of their deceased spouses' benefits.

While you have no say in the amount of benefits you are due, you can decide at what age you would like to start collecting benefits. Generally speaking, the sooner you start taking it (the earliest age you're eligible is 62), the smaller your benefit will be. The longer you delay (up to the age of 70), the bigger it'll be, but the longer you'll have to live in order for it to make economic sense.

ASK THE EXPERTS

How much can I expect to get?

The amount of your monthly check will be based on your birth date, the age you start collecting, and the average amount of money you have earned over your lifetime. There is a limit on benefits. In 2002 it was about $1,600 per month for someone at full retirement age. (And yes, in some cases your Social Security can be taxed. See page 98 for more.) To see how much you'll get, look at your Personal Earnings & Benefit Estimate Statement (PES), which the Social Security Administration annually mails to everyone over age 25. This shows how much in annual Social Security benefits you'll get if you **1.** retire early, **2.** retire late, **3.** retire at your normal retirement age, or **4.** become disabled.

I didn't get my Social Security Personal Earnings & Benefit Estimate. How do I request one?

You have several options:

● Call the SSA at 800-772-1213 to request the statement.

● Get a copy of the request form at your local Social Security office. Then fill it out and mail it in.

● Submit your request on the Social Security Administration's Web site, **www.ssa.gov**, either directly on-screen or by downloading a request form and mailing it in.

There's an error in my PES. What should I do?

If you spot a mistake, contact the SSA immediately to have their estimate adjusted. Waiting more than a year or two to correct errors can make the corrections difficult to achieve. To contact SSA:

Tel: 800-772-1213

Internet: **www.ssa.gov**

E-mail: webmaster@ssa.gov

HOW ARE BENEFITS CALCULATED

Your benefits aren't tied to how much in SS taxes you've paid. In fact, the SS taxes you've paid don't actually accumulate for your benefit—they've been used for retirement benefits of current retirees. The system is set up so that your own SS benefits will come from SS taxes paid by people who are still working when you retire.

The way your benefits are calculated is so complicated that not even your genius Uncle Mort could understand it: things like "average indexed monthly earnings," "computation years," "divisor months," "bend points," and "primary insurance amounts" go into the computation. Luckily, the computers at the Social Security Administration (SSA) do the work for you.

when to start taking your *benefits*

Waiting for full benefits

"FULL" RETIREMENT AGE USED to be 65 for everyone. But thanks to greater life expectancies, the government has moved the official year back a bit. Depending on your birthday, full retirement ranges from 65 to 67. The chart below indicates the age when you are eligible for full retirement SS benefits.

If your birthday is:	Then your "full" retirement age is:
1-1-38 or before	65
1-2-38 to 1-1-39	65 and 2 months
1-2-39 to 1-1-40	65 and 4 months
1-2-40 to 1-1-41	65 and 6 months
1-2-41 to 1-1-42	65 and 8 months
1-2-42 to 1-1-43	65 and 10 months
1-2-43 to 1-1-55	66
1-2-55 to 1-1-56	66 and 2 months
1-2-56 to 1-1-57	66 and 4 months
1-2-57 to 1-1-58	66 and 6 months
1-2-58 to 1-1-59	66 and 8 months
1-2-59 to 1-1-60	66 and 10 months
After 1-1-60	67

You can start your SS benefits as early as age 62. But there's a catch: The amount you get each month will be 20 percent to 30 percent less than if you wait until your full retirement age.

You can delay your benefits, too. The longer you wait, the higher your monthly benefit is likely to be. Depending on your year of birth, the amount will be 3 percent to 8 percent more per year than it would be at full retirement. (Once you turn 70, the amount won't keep increasing, but you can still file for benefits.)

ASK THE EXPERTS

I don't know what to do—should I take my Social Security early or wait until I reach full retirement?

Here are some things to consider when making this decision.

1. Your health and life expectancy. If you're healthy and your family routinely lives into the triple digits, delaying SS could be beneficial, since you'll probably have ample years of higher earning to make up for taking fewer total payments. On the other hand, if you are in poor health, taking SS benefits earlier and maximizing the number of payments you receive might make the most sense.

2. Your work situation. If you keep working after you retire, taking early benefits could cost you. How? If you earn more than $11,000 a year, your benefits will be reduced $1 for every $2 you earn above the limit, until you reach full retirement age (see page 82).

3. Your marital status. If you have a younger spouse with low earnings, waiting as long as possible might be best because it will ensure a greater income source to your spouse, even after you have passed away.

4. Your feelings. Some people simply feel more comfortable starting their retirement benefits as soon as possible, even if it means less total income overall. If you feel it's best to take the "bird in hand," then go for it.

applying for *benefits*

SO, YOU'VE DECIDED TO TAKE the leap and apply for Social Security benefits. That's great! Now what?

First, try to apply at least three months before you want your benefits to start, because it takes at least eight weeks for your application to be processed. If you're not sure whether to apply early, on time, or delayed, or if you have other questions or concerns, contacting the SSA six months beforehand is a good idea.

The checks won't start coming until you've signed up

When you sign up for Social Security at age 65, you will automatically be enrolled in Medicare. If you don't plan to apply for SS by your 65th birthday, contact the Social Security Association for Medicare enrollment at least three months before you turn 65 and apply for Medicare separately.

There are several ways to apply for Social Security benefits: over the phone, in person, or online. To prevent delays, avoid filing more than one application (online *and* over the phone, for instance).

- Call 800-772-1213 to schedule a time to apply over the phone.
- Call 800-772-1213 to schedule a time to apply at a nearby Social Security office.
- To apply for benefits online, go to the Social Security Web site: **www.ssa.gov/applytoretire**.
- You can't apply for benefits by mail, but you can write for assistance. Address your questions to: SSA, Office of Public Inquiries, 6401 Security Blvd., Room 4-C-D Annex, Baltimore, MD 21235.

 **SK THE EXPERTS**

What documents do I need to have on hand before I can apply for Social Security?

Get ready for a shock. The examiners at the Social Security office will need to check all of the following documents:

- Social Security number
- Original birth certificate
- Original W-2 forms or self-employment tax return for the last two years
- Military discharge papers
- Spouse's birth certificate and Social Security number
- Proof of U.S. citizenship or lawful alien status (if you weren't born in the U.S.)
- Bank account name and number (so your benefits can be directly deposited into your account)
- A marriage certificate if you are applying for benefits based on your spouse's earnings
- A death certificate if you and your family want to apply for survivor's benefits

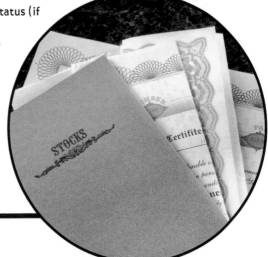

TIMELY TIP: WHEN TO GO

Plan your visit to the local SSA office at the end of a month, going three and a half months before your full retirement date if necessary. Why? Most checks are paid the first few days of the month, and people usually request lost/replacement checks the first two weeks of the month, so you'll probably sit in the waiting room longer if you go early in the month. And avoid lunchtime visits, since there are more working people looking for help—and fewer aides there to give it.

taxes on your *benefits*

OKAY, NOW FOR THE BAD NEWS. The Social Security benefits you receive may be subject to federal income taxes. The amount of your Social Security benefit that will be taxed depends on your adjusted gross income, including *half* of your Social Security benefit, and any tax-exempt dividends or interest. **Adjusted gross income** is your income after you've taken certain deductions, such as retirement plan contributions, alimony, and moving expenses.

If you owe taxes on your Social Security benefits, you will need to pay them in **estimated quarterly payments** (see page 32) or have the amount of tax you owe withheld from your Social Security check. Although you'll get a smaller check each month, you won't have to remember to make your quarterly payments. It's kind of like the old days of getting a paycheck with the taxes already taken out.

The amount depends on your other sources of income

An estimation of the federal taxes on your Social Security benefits appears below:

ESTIMATING TAXES ON SOCIAL SECURITY BENEFITS

Income including one-half of your Social Security benefits		Tax consequences on benefits:
If you're single	**If you're married**	
Up to $25,000	Up to $32,000 combined income	Social Security not taxed
Between $25,000 and $34,000	Between $32,000 and $44,000	50 percent of Social Security taxed
Over $34,000	Over $44,000	Up to 85 percent of Social Security taxed

NOW WHERE DO I GO?!

I want to continue working after I retire. Will my salary affect my Social Security payment?

It depends. As of January 2000, once you reach your full retirement age, you can earn as much as you want without anything being deducted from your Social Security benefits. However, you will be penalized for working if you take benefits before your full retirement age, provided the amount you earn annually is more than $11,000 (the cap for 2002). For every $2 you earn above that amount, you will forfeit $1 in Social Security benefits. During the year you reach full retirement age, you will forfeit $1 for every $3 you earn annually over $30,000. Beginning with the month you reach full retirement, you no longer forfeit any amount, no matter how much you earn.

How can I boost my Social Security benefits?

If you delay taking your Social Security benefits after your full retirement age, you could increase the amount of benefits you eventually receive—provided your earnings remain high. Since your benefit is determined in part by an average of your highest earnings, several more high-income years could bring up that average a bit. But remember that no matter how high your income was, there is a set maximum limit to Social Security payments.

FIRST PERSON DISASTER STORY

Giving Money Back to Uncle Sam

I wanted to retire as soon as possible (I can live on the interest from my investments), so I applied for Social Security benefits the minute I turned 62. Six months later, I was offered an interesting part-time job, paid by the hour, at the museum where I used to be a curator. I got to meet lots of fascinating people who were donors, as well as attending special events at their homes. Before I knew it, I was piling up the hours and ended up making $30,000 a year from the job. I was horrified to find that my Social Security benefits would be reduced by $1 for every $2 that I had I earned over $11,000. Since I only got $13,750 a year from Social Security, and was penalized $9,500, it wiped out 70 percent of my SS benefits. I would have been smarter to wait until I was 65 to take my Social Security benefits. Then I could have earned as much as I wanted with no penalty, and my Social Security checks would have been about 20 percent fatter as well.

—**George L., New York, New York**

social security and your *family*

Who else might receive checks based on your benefits?

YOU MAY NOT BE THE ONLY ONE who reaps Social Security rewards from your lifetime of slaving away. Your spouse may be at an advantage if *half* your benefit amount is higher than her full benefit amount. At age 62, your non-working spouse is entitled to a reduced benefit (37.5 percent of your full benefit), *as long as you are already collecting your benefits*. If she waits until her full retirement age, she will be entitled to 50 percent of your full benefit. (Similar benefits apply to your unmarried ex-spouse, provided your marriage lasted more than 10 years, during which you worked and earned your Social Security credits.)

Social Security also helps your family after you die. Your spouse will continue to get Social Security, based on your benefit amount. (If your spouse worked, Social Security will base your benefits on the higher amount of the two of you.) Your ex-spouse will still continue to collect on your Social Security after you die. And thanks to your working years, Social Security will pay monthly survivor benefits to any minor children (under age 19), and any disabled children age 18 or older. Even your elderly parents are covered, provided they have been dependent upon you for at least half of their financial support.

By the way, if you're retiring and your current and/or ex-spouse has substantially higher lifetime earnings than you, you may be able to boost your own benefit by making a claim on his or her account.

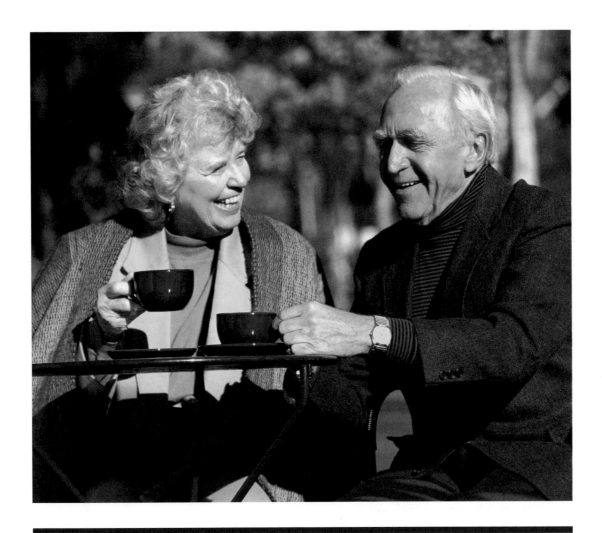

DISABILITY INSURANCE

If you're not yet at full retirement age but become fully disabled, you may receive benefits from Social Security through Social Security Disability Insurance. Like Social Security, the amount you receive will be based on the number of credits you have earned and the amount of money you made during your working years. Start the application process immediately after you are told you won't be able to work again, because the approval process sometimes takes months. If you are turned down on your first try, you may want to gather more medical evidence and try again.

Disability Insurance from Social Security does not apply if you become disabled *after* you reach full retirement age. See page 138 (long-term care insurance) and page 130 (Medicare) for more information.

now what do I do?

Answers to common questions

If I delay taking my Social Security benefits past full retirement age, will my Medicare benefits be delayed, too?

No. Even if you decide to delay your retirement benefits, you can—and generally should—sign up for Medicare at age 65.

I've worked for many years, but my Social Security statement doesn't reflect any of my earnings. What happened?

There are a number of people who aren't covered by Social Security. These include federal employees hired before 1984; workers covered under the Railroad Retirement System; state employees covered under their own retirement system; many school system employees with their own programs; and certain members of the clergy who elect not to participate in Social Security. If you're not covered, you probably haven't had SS taxes withheld from your paycheck, but check with the SSA to be sure.

My husband passed away several years ago, and I'm thinking about remarrying. How will this impact my Social Security benefits?

It depends. If you're already collecting as a widow on your deceased husband's account, your benefits will not change when you remarry. However, if you are just now preparing to file for widow's benefits (you are eligible at age 60), file before you get remarried—otherwise you won't be eligible for the benefits.

When will I receive my check each month?

Checks are paid once a month, in arrears. For example, your payment for your April benefits will arrive in May, depending on your birthday:

IF YOUR BIRTHDAY IS:	YOUR PAYMENT IS MADE:
1st through 10th of the month	2nd Wednesday of each month
11th through 20th of the month	3rd Wednesday of each month
21st through 31st of the month	4th Wednesday of each month

To access your money as soon as possible, sign up for the government's direct deposit program when you apply. Funds will be posted to your checking account and available to you the same day.

If I've earned a million dollars, will my Social Security benefit reflect that?

The Social Security Administration has set a maximum income level (which increases slightly every year due to inflation). Once you exceed that level, the benefit paid by Social Security stays the same. For example, if billionaire Bill Gates (born in 1955) starts taking Social Security benefits at age 66, the amount he gets will be exactly the same as that received by all other people born that year whose lifetime earnings are at least at the maximum level.

I've worked a total of nine years. Do I qualify for Social Security benefits?

No, not unless you're married and your spouse qualifies, and you can secure benefits under his or her earnings. The criterion for qualifying is 40 credits, and you can't earn more than 4 credits per year, regardless of how much money you have made. That's why it's important to review your Social Security Earnings & Benefit Estimate before you retire. Working one more year could make all the difference toward a happy retirement.

NOW WHERE DO I GO?!

WEB ADDRESSES	PUBLICATIONS
www.ssa.gov (800-772-1213) www.socialsecurity.com/opening.html	**Benefits Handbook** By Stanley A. Tomkiel III

401(k)s
and pensions

" *I'm afraid I'll run out of money.*
How much can I safely withdraw
from my 401(k) each year? "

your
401(k)

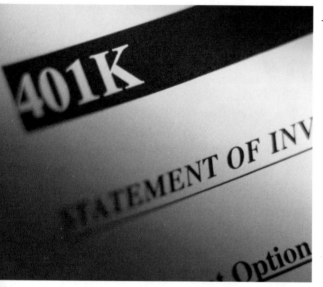

How much is in there?

FINALLY YOU'RE RETIRING, AND
it's time to start withdrawing the money from
your 401(k). Hurrah! How much have you got
in there anyway? It depends on these factors:

● **THE AMOUNT OF MONEY YOU CON-
TRIBUTED FROM EACH PAYCHECK AND THE
NUMBER OF YEARS YOU CONTRIBUTED TO
THE PLAN:** You, the employee, saved a fixed
percentage of your weekly paycheck in a tax-
deferred retirement savings account. But you
may have saved less than the maximum. You
may have changed the percentage during your
working years or gone without making a contri-
bution part of the time. If you got in a pinch, you may even have had to
borrow from your account, which means less was invested, so less was
earned. Those decisions were left up to you. Now you will find they have
affected the amount in your account.

● **THE SIZE OF YOUR EMPLOYER'S CONTRIBUTION (IF ANY):** Your
company may have made contributions to your account as well, depending on the company's policy. For every pretax dollar you contributed (up
to a certain percentage), your employer may have kicked in anywhere
from $.25 to $1.00 (referred to as the **matching amount**).

● **THE TYPES OF INVESTMENTS YOU PICKED AND HOW THOSE
INVESTMENTS PERFORMED OVER TIME:** The 401(k) allows some discretion in how your account is invested. The amount your account has
earned is dependent in part on how well those investments performed
over the years.

● **DON'T FORGET ABOUT TAXES:** Your 401(k) contribution was made with pretax dollars. That means the money was deducted from your paycheck before taxes were withdrawn. And you've paid no taxes so far on what your 401(k) account has earned. The manner in which you take the money out of your account will determine how and when you eventually pay the taxes on the money.

ASK THE EXPERTS

Doesn't all the money in my 401(k) account belong to me?

It depends. That part of the money you contributed from your paycheck, and its earnings, are yours—period. It doesn't matter if you worked for the company for five weeks or five years. The matching contribution that your employer kicked in, however, is a different matter. This money isn't yours until you are **vested**, or officially entitled to it. Many employers allow you to vest in increments over a period of seven years; some offer immediate vesting. Others vest you all at once, but after a set period of time. Check with your employee benefits office about the vesting requirements for receiving the company's contributions before you make any retirement decisions.

Could a former employer owe me any money?

Yes, if you've switched jobs and left your 401(k) account invested with a previous employer, you're entitled to the amount you contributed and the money it has continued to earn. Contact your former company's benefits department and see what's coming to you.

I am so tempted to take the money and buy a round-the-world trip. Is this a good way to spend it?

Not unless you want to get hit with a huge tax bill. There are rules about when you can begin taking out 401(k) money, as well as how much you should take out in order to avoid tax problems.

401(k):
lump-sum
distribution

Get your hands on that money

OVER THE YEARS, YOU'VE REGULARLY SOCKED away those pretax dollars into your 401(k) account. Good work! You can now reap the rewards. Whether it's worth $10,000 or $1 million, those retirement savings are finally yours. It's time to think about how you're going to take it out. Most people take it in one lump sum. The careful ones consider the tax consequences. Read on and find out.

TAKE THE MONEY AND RUN This idea sounds better than it actually is. Why? When you take a lump-sum payment, you get all of the money at once, within one tax year. Trouble is, you have to pay all the income tax due on that money in the same tax year, so you'll have to fork over a hefty chunk of your savings to the government almost immediately. What's more, the tax-deferred earnings on your money will stop.

TAKE THE MONEY AND ROLL IT INTO AN IRA This strategy generally makes the most sense. When you roll your 401(k) distribution into an Individual Retirement Account (see page 116), your money can continue to grow tax-deferred. You maintain control over the money, investing your account as aggressively or as conservatively as you want. And you can tap into the money as needed.

LEAVE IT WITH YOUR COMPANY—AND DON'T DO A THING If you leave the money in your 401(k) until you make a final decision, the company's investment firm will continue to invest it according to your wishes, and you can withdraw what you want, when you want (see page 98). Just make sure your spouse and heirs know about the account.

HOW DO I ROLL OVER MY 401(k)?

You have several options. But the IRS has some sticky rules. Be prepared for some paperwork and a short time frame (60 days) within which you need to complete the task.

1) DO IT DIRECTLY: Tell your employer to deposit your lump sum directly into a new or an existing IRA, if you already have one set up. For a direct rollover, your employer will ask you to fill out an instruction form indicating exactly where the money should go, such as to a particular mutual fund. The advantages: You beat the IRS requirement that says your employer must deduct a withholding tax from your lump sum, because the check isn't made out to you, it's made out to the institution. In many cases, the check will be sent directly to your house, in which case you'll need to mail it to your IRA's custodian. As long as this check is made out to the IRA account, it'll be considered a "direct rollover."

2) DO IT YOURSELF WITHIN 60 DAYS: Your employer hands over a lump-sum check to you. Now you've got 60 days to roll over the money into an IRA. The disadvantages: Since the check is made out to you, your employer must deduct 20 percent mandatory withholding tax, which means you'll only have a check for 80 percent of your money. You'll eventually get a refund for that 20 percent, of course, when you file your tax return. But meanwhile, during the 60-day rollover time limit, you'll have to add the missing 20 percent out of your own pocket *or that 20 percent will be taxed as income.* Another drawback: Miss that 60-day deadline, even by a hair, and you'll owe tax on the *entire amount.*

3) CONVERT IT TO A ROTH IRA: This is a bit tricky. First, you roll your 401(k) fund into a traditional IRA. Then you convert that IRA into a Roth (see page 120). There are no limits on the amount you can convert, but there are eligibility limits based on income. If you convert, you may want to do it in smaller increments because the taxes that you will have to pay upon conversion can strain your cash flow. But from that point on, all of your withdrawals, both principal and interest, will generally be completely free from income tax. Why convert? Because you have a lot of retirement funding and you don't want to bother with mandatory withdrawals, and the whole Roth IRA can be left to your heirs income tax free.

401(k):
leave it with your employer

*If their
401(k) plan
is giving
you good
returns, let
the money
stay there*

IT'S TRUE, MANY PEOPLE PREFER to take all their 401(k) money with them at retirement. But you do have another, very smart option: Just leave your 401(k) where it is. Here are several reasons why it might make sense for you:

YOU DON'T WANT TO MAKE FURTHER INVESTMENT DECISIONS RIGHT NOW. Perhaps you like the way the funds in your company plan are performing, or you enjoy the investment options offered by your plan. Why reinvent the wheel by taking the money out and then spending time looking for a suitable investment for it somewhere else?

YOU WANT YOUR MONEY TO CONTINUE TO GROW TAX-DEFERRED. Leaving the money in your employer's plan has no immediate tax consequences. Your money will keep growing tax-deferred. You'll only pay tax on the money as you withdraw it, the same as with an IRA.

YOU'RE UNSURE ABOUT WHAT TO DO WITH YOUR MONEY. Doing nothing can be okay in this instance, while you take the time to think things over. Leave your money in your 401(k) account . . . and mull over your options for a few months. Should you decide a month from now—or several years from now—that you want to roll the money into an IRA, you can do so at that time.

 **SK THE EXPERTS**

I'd like to receive a monthly income from my 401 (k). How do I do that?

Here are two ways to do it:

1. Take a lump-sum distribution and roll it immediately into an IRA. You can then take monthly payments—or more or less frequent distributions—as you see fit. For example, a mutual fund company (when acting as the custodian of your Rollover IRA) will let you set up an automatic distribution plan. That is, they'll automatically mail you a monthly check.

2. Ask your company to set up an installment payment schedule. Your employer (or the mutual fund that manages the company's 401(k) plan) will essentially use your money to pay you a set monthly amount immediately. (These are called **annuitized distributions**.) This guarantees you a fixed income for the rest of your life.

I like the idea of getting annuitized distributions from my company, but is it the best way to go?

Ask your financial planner or accountant about the long-term implications. An annuitized distribution is safe, and it's easy—you don't have to lift a finger to get your money. However, an annuity is not generally the most economical choice, because it offers no protection against **inflation** (the rising cost of living). Rolling over the money into an IRA is considered a better bet because the investments usually produce higher total returns than if you annuitize. Bear in mind that once you annuitize, you can't go back. That is, if you decide at some future date that rolling over the money into an IRA would have been a smarter option, you can't switch.

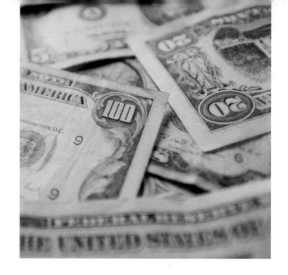

401(k): required distributions

Once you start taking them, you have to keep on taking them every year

IF YOU DIDN'T ROLL OVER THE MONEY from your 401(k) into an IRA, and you want or need to start taking money out, there are a few rules to follow. Starting at age 59½, you can take as much or as little money out of your 401(k) as you want—just know you will have to pay income tax on it. Or you can wait to start taking distributions at any year up until age 70½, when you absolutely *must* start taking something called a **required minimum distribution** (or RMD).

How is the required minimum distribution determined? Good question. Basically, your 401(k) balance is divided by a figure from a government distribution table. (It's actually an actuarial table based on the life expectancies of you and your beneficiary.) Here's another rule: Once you start taking your RMDs, you cannot stop. Every year thereafter, you have to take at least your minimum distribution. You can, of course, take out more than your required minimum distribution. Just check with your accountant to see if the extra income will move you into an undesirable tax bracket.

The one exception to the RMD rule? If you don't retire by 70½ and continue working, you don't have to take the minimum withdrawals from your 401(k). And you can keep making contributions until the year you actually do retire—welcome news for those who want to put off their retirement.

 **SK THE EXPERTS**

I'm 55 and want to retire early. Can I get the money out of my 401(k) early?

Yes. There is an early retirement loophole that lets you take money out starting at age 55 provided you are retiring from a job with the same company that has your 401(k).

I was laid off at 54. Can I take money out of my 401(k) without paying a penalty?

Alas, you'll get socked with a 10 percent early withdrawal penalty in addition to the usual income taxes—unless your withdrawal qualifies as a hardship withdrawal, such as the purchase of a new home or the cost of a college education, or a "special circumstance" such as substantial medical expenses and early retirement. Check with the IRS or your accountant first to make sure you qualify.

Your SEP, SIMPLE, or *keogh*

Distributions work like those for IRAs and 401(k)s

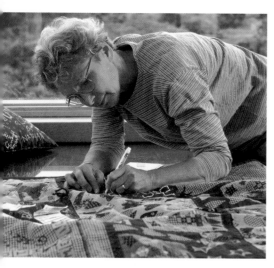

IF YOU'VE WORKED FOR SMALL COMPANIES or been self-employed for most of your working life, chances are you have a SEP IRA (Simplified Employee Pension Plan), SIMPLE IRA, or Keogh retirement plan ready and waiting for your self-appointed day of retirement. And today's the day. But how do you take the money out? Are there rules and regulations?

Yes, whenever taxes are involved, there are rules. The distribution rules for SEPs and SIMPLEs are fairly, well, simple. They are subject to the same basic rules as a regular IRA. That is, you can start taking money out of your SEP or SIMPLE when you turn age 59½—and of course, you must pay income tax on it (usually at a lower income tax bracket now that you've stopped working). One more rule: You must start making a **required minimum distribution** (or RMD) withdrawal the year that you turn 70½. (Technically, you have until April 1 of the year *after* you turn 70½ to begin withdrawing the funds.) As with IRAs, your RMD amount is based on the life expectancies of you and your beneficiary.

Taking your money out of a Keogh is the same deal. Turn 59½ and you can start taking it out and paying taxes (hopefully at a lower income tax rate than when you were working). Once you turn 70½ you must start taking it out—unless you keep working. Here a Keogh is like a 401(k): If you keep working in your same line of work, you don't have to take any RMDs and in fact, you can continue to make contributions. Good news for the working diehards.

 **SK THE EXPERTS**

Do I have to take minimum distributions from my Simplified Employee Pension (SEP) if I'm still working?

Yes. SEP IRAs and SIMPLE IRAs operate under the same rules as regular IRAs. You must start taking money out of your account in the year that you turn 70½. It doesn't matter if you are still working or not. Uncle Sam wants his taxes paid back.

Are there any special rules for early withdrawals of SIMPLEs?

Yes. If you make an early withdrawal of funds from your SIMPLE within two years of the date that you began contributing to it, you'll have to pay an early withdrawal penalty of 25 percent. After two years, the penalty drops to 10 percent.

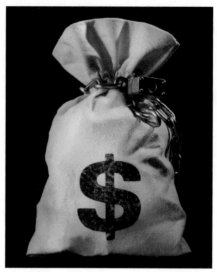

your *pension*

Many larger companies still offer them

AH, THE PENSION. It used to be standard for workers to receive pension payments once they retired. Now it seems more like found money. If you are **vested** (entitled to certain benefits based on years of service) and due pension money, good for you. The amount you will receive is calculated by a formula, which varies from one employer to the next. Typically, it includes factors such as the number of years you worked for the company and your final salary, or an average of your salary over a number of years when it was highest, or a flat amount per year of service.

How much you get will depend on when you retire: early, late, or at the normal retirement age. If you're retiring early (after a long career with the company), for instance, your pension benefits may be reduced because you'll now be receiving them over a longer period of time. And if you've been with the firm for just a few years (after job-hopping most of your career), your pension benefits may not amount to much at all.

How much you get will also depend on how you collect your pension benefits once you retire. Some companies allow you to take the money in one lump sum and invest it yourself (see page 108), or as an annuity, collecting a monthly check from the company for the rest of your life (see pages 106–107).

ASK THE EXPERTS

Do I have to worry about vesting?

Absolutely. In order to collect a pension, you must be fully vested (that is, eligible to receive pension benefits) in your company's plan. How do you become eligible? Companies have different vesting schedules. With some firms, you're vested immediately upon employment; with others, you're vested gradually over a period of years (known as graded vesting), or all at once after a certain time period has elapsed, say five years (known as cliff vesting). If you are not fully vested, some companies offer to vest you as an incentive to take early retirement. Check with your employee benefits office to find out about your company's vesting schedule.

I keep hearing about something called "defined benefits." What does that mean?

It means that the amount you receive from your pension plan is a set amount for the rest of your life. An annuity-type distribution is considered a defined benefit plan.

Are taxes taken out of my pension check?

In most cases, the money that you receive from your pension is considered taxable income. That means, obviously, that you must pay income tax on the money. Will those taxes be taken directly from your monthly check? It depends on your particular plan. Plans typically withhold taxes from your check, but you can usually opt not to have the taxes withheld. In the latter case, you'll then have to pay those taxes yourself, on an annual or quarterly basis. Before you retire and start drawing your pension, ask about the tax implications of your particular plan and what arrangements, if any, are made for tax withholding.

pension annuity payments

Choosing the right type may be tricky

IF YOU DECIDE TO TAKE YOUR ANNUAL PENSION benefits in a monthly annuity distribution, you'll have to make one more big decision: You must choose between a **single-life annuity** (the payments stop when you die) or a **joint and survivor annuity** (you get a smaller monthly income, but it continues to be paid to your spouse after your death).

Before you decide, ask your company's pension office for an estimate of both amounts, and discuss the issue with your spouse and your financial adviser. Keep in mind that your choice is generally irrevocable. That means once you retire and start receiving pension benefits of one type, you can't then ask the company to change to the other type of payment.

Single-Life Annuity This provides a monthly amount to you alone, the retiree, for life. When you pick this option, your monthly payments will be larger because the benefits are based on your life expectancy alone. The downside: Your spouse will be left with no income from your pension when you die. If you're not married, then you should take the single-life option and get the higher payments. If you and your spouse each have solid pensions of your own—and your spouse won't have to depend on your pension for support after you die—then, again, go with the larger, single-life annuity. But if your spouse might need that pension money after you die, then select the joint and survivor annuity.

Joint and Survivor Annuity This type of payment provides a monthly income to you, the retiree. When you die, however, your pension keeps on issuing monthly payments to your spouse for the rest of his or her life. The drawback: You get less money each month than you would with the single-life option because your pension benefit must now be spread over the life expectancies of two people.

RED FLAG

Your spouse is entitled to survivor rights to your pension. In most cases, that means when you die your spouse will get at least half the pension benefit that you were receiving. When you elect a single-life option, however, you waive that right. Under most plans, your spouse must sign an agreement form indicating that he or she consents to the terms of a single-life annuity.

ASK THE EXPERTS

What's the better choice: Single-Life or Joint and Survivor?

The answer depends on your personal situation. Married women are typically advised to take single-life payment on their own pensions because women generally outlive men. Conversely, husbands are often advised to take the joint and survivor option on their pensions because statistics indicate that their wives will probably outlive them. With this arrangement, the husband gets less money each month than he would with the single-life option. When the husband dies, his spouse will get a monthly payment for the rest of her life. But the surviving spouse does not get as much as the retiree received during his life. The surviving spouse generally gets 50 percent of the original benefit.

Can I name my child as my beneficiary?

The joint and survivor option is for your spouse only. If you are widowed or single, you may be able to take other options. (Again, this depends on your plan.) One such option is called a Guaranteed Payment Annuity, which lets you pick another family member as beneficiary.

I'm divorced. Am I entitled to half of my ex-husband's pension?

A pension is a marital asset, so if pension payments were not stipulated in your divorce proceedings, you can't get them now.

FIRST PERSON · DISASTER STORY

Sometimes Conventional Wisdom Doesn't Work

When I retired five years ago, I chose the joint and survivor benefit for my pension. It was the conventional thing to do. I didn't take my wife's poor health into consideration. I guess I always assumed she would outlive me, and so I wanted to provide for her. She passed away last year, and now I'm stuck with these lower benefits for the rest of my life. I wish I had thought about the decision a bit harder and taken the single-life option. An old colleague of mine told me that not only should I have taken the single-life option, but I could have used the extra money from the higher payment to help continue to make payments on my whole-life insurance policy. That way, if I died first, my wife would collect on the policy. And if she died first, I could cancel the policy and I'd still be getting the higher pension payments. Live and learn.

—Sam S., Cleveland, Ohio

pension: lump-sum payment

Invested well, it can protect against inflation

WHEN YOU RETIRE, YOUR EMPLOYER may offer to give you your pension in one single check. This is called a **lump-sum payment**. Instead of getting a monthly income paid for the rest of your life, you get the entire amount rolled over into a separate or existing IRA. Then it becomes your job to invest the money—and/or spend it—as you see fit.

The amount you get is calculated using a slightly different formula than the monthly payment plan. It's based on the following: the amount of the single-life annuity; the retiree's age; and an interest rate, determined by the plan, that will convert your possible future pension income into a current market value.

Not all pensions offer this alternative. But if your pension plan does, you'll want to consider the following:

● Can you invest that money wisely (or perhaps pay someone to do it for you)? Lump sums make sense for people who believe that they can earn more by investing their money themselves than they would have otherwise received in monthly annuity payments.

● How badly do you think inflation will erode your savings? A lump-sum payment invested partially in stocks should protect your money against rising prices. Most annuities offer no such protection.

Talk to a financial planner or an accountant who can run the numbers for you. Before you can make an intelligent decision, you need to see how each choice stacks up over the long term.

PENSION CHECKLIST

Important questions to ask your company benefits administrator about your pension plan:

- Is the pension plan "integrated" with your Social Security benefits? Under this arrangement, your monthly pension income would be reduced once you start collecting Social Security benefits. The amount of your monthly Social Security benefit would be subtracted from your original pension benefit, and you would receive the reduced monthly amount from the company.
- How will your benefits be calculated? Different plans use different formulas. A **unit benefit formula**, for instance, typically works like this: 1 percent to 2 percent multiplied by your final average compensation (which is usually your average compensation over the highest 3 or 5 years within the last 10 years, but it could also be your career average compensation) multiplied by your years of service. A **fixed benefit formula**, on the other hand, usually works this way: After 25 years of service, you get 50 percent of your final average compensation.
- If you retire early—even two years early—will your benefits be affected? If so, by how much? The pension plan administrator will usually give you comparative estimates a few years before your full retirement date.
- At retirement, can you take your payment as a lump sum or as an annuity with monthly payments? Not all companies offer the option of a lump-sum payout. (If your pension benefit is small, will it be paid annually instead of monthly?)
- Are your benefits going to be adjusted for inflation? Less than 10 percent of corporate pension plans adjust annuity payments for inflation. When making a decision whether to collect your pension as a lump sum for you to invest, you'll have to consider that, by investing a part of it in equities, you can make up for the rate of inflation. Your financial adviser can determine how much should be put into equities to make this happen.

IN CASE QUESTIONS ARISE IN THE FUTURE

You will need to know the name of your pension plan, the Employer Identification Number (EIN) and the plan's number (PN). Why? It makes applying for your pension a snap. Also, sometimes companies merge and pensions can get lost in the shuffle. If you've "lost" your pension, contact the Pension Benefit Guaranty Corp. at 800-400-7242 or **www. pbgc.gov**.

now what do I do?

Answers to common questions

I borrowed money from my 401(k) account. Since this is technically my own money, why should I bother to repay the loan before retirement?

Taxes. Taxes. Taxes. When you retire and leave your job, any outstanding loans against your 401(k) generally come due immediately (or, in some cases, within 60 days). If you can't pay the money back—or you simply choose not to—your loan will be considered a premature withdrawal. You'll then owe the taxes due on that amount, plus an early-withdrawal penalty. If you're under age 59½, you'll get zapped with the 10 percent early-withdrawal penalty and you will have to pay income tax on what you borrowed.

My company lost several of its key clients in the past two years. If my company goes out of business or declares bankruptcy, will I lose my pension benefits?

Probably not. Until 1974, there was little or no protection for pensions. But thanks to the Employee Retirement Income Security Act (ERISA), most pension plans are now insured by the federal government through the Pension Benefit Guaranty Corporation (PBGC). If your employer goes out of business or cannot afford to pay your retirement benefits, PBGC will pay your benefits, up to certain limits. In most cases, though, the PBGC guarantee covers all of the earned benefits.

I can't decide if I should take my pension in a lump sum or as a monthly payment. What do most people do?

Everyone's situation is slightly different, but here are two general rules of thumb: 1) If you're an experienced investor, or if you work with a good financial planner, consider the lump sum. The interest rates offered by company-sponsored annuities generally aren't that competitive, and you can do better by investing the lump sum. 2) If you're an inexperienced investor or have no trusted financial adviser, consider the monthly pension. Yes, you might be able to earn more by investing the money yourself, but then again, you might not. At least with the pension, you know what you're getting—and it's for life.

I'm a doctor working in a not-for-profit hospital. I've always contributed to our hospital's 403(b) plan, which works something like a 401(k). Are the rules for mandatory withdrawals the same?

Not necessarily. There were no withdrawal rules when 403(b) plans were first set up. But the Tax Reform Act of 1986 decreed that 403(b)s should have distribution rules like 401(k) plans. In other words, you must start taking money out at age 70½. There are some loopholes in this new ruling, though, which might allow you to defer withdrawals until age 75. Check with a financial planner or a pension expert.

I'm afraid that I'll run out of money eventually. How much can I safely withdraw from my 401(k) each year?

How much you can safely withdraw—without fear of depleting all your funds—depends on a number of factors, such as your other sources of retirement income, your life expectancy, and your general living expenses. Some recent studies have found, however, that you'd be pretty safe if your annual withdrawal is no more than 4 percent of the value of your 401(k).

NOW WHERE DO I GO?!

WEB ADDRESSES	PUBLICATIONS
www.aoa.dhhs.gov/factsheets/pension.html The Administration on Aging offers information about pensions and "pension counseling programs" to help you obtain the correct information about your pension plan.	**IRAs, 401(k)s & Other Retirement Plans: Taking Your Money Out** by Twila Slesnick, Ph.D., Enrolled Agent and John C. Suttle, CPA
www.401K.com A Fidelity site, it answers many questions about 401(k) plans.	**The Complete Idiot's Guide to 401(k) Plans** by Wayne G. Bogosian and Dee Lee
www.lifeadvice.org MetLife offers information on a variety of personal finance topics, such as "401(k) Plans" and "Planning for Retirement."	**A Commonsense Guide to Your 401(k)** by Mary Rowland
www.quicken.com A compendium of understandable personal finance information. Click on Retirement.	**Making the Most of Your 401(k)** by Gordon K. Williamson

dealing with
IRAs

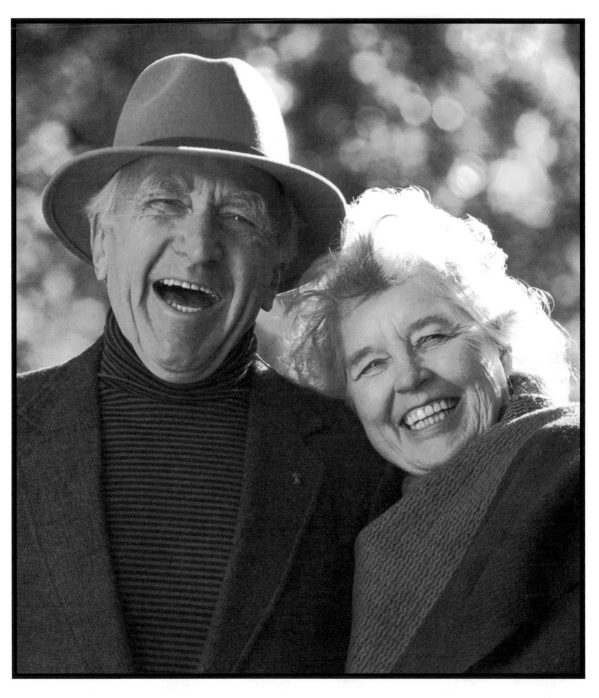

" *How do we go about beginning the withdrawal process for our IRAs?* "

your accounts and *taxes*

Each type serves a different purpose

IF YOU'VE DECIDED TO RETIRE, then you've probably accumulated a nest egg from years of work-oriented savings programs, such as a 401(k) or a Keogh. But what about money you saved on your own? It's time to take a look at all these various personal accounts and decide which ones you want to keep once you're retired. Here's a rundown on those accounts and their pros and cons, as well as their tax implications.

BANK CHECKING/SAVINGS/MONEY MARKET ACCOUNTS Checking accounts are handy for check-writing, debit cards, ATM machines, and teller access. Savings and money market accounts earn interest on short-term savings. *Pro:* Accounts offered by banks and savings and loans are all federally insured. (A money market account from a brokerage house is not usually federally insured.) *Con:* Any interest they pay won't keep up with the average annual rate of inflation, and they charge various service fees that can add up. *Taxes:* Any interest these accounts earn is taxed at your ordinary income tax rate.

CERTIFICATES OF DEPOSIT (CDs) These are contracts a bank makes with you to pay interest for the use of your money over a period of time, say three months to several years. *Pro:* They're federally insured. *Con:* Early withdrawals incur a penalty, and interest may just barely cover inflation (averaging 3.3 percent over the past 80 years). *Taxes:* Although you don't actually receive any interest until the term ends, you do pay income tax out of your own pocket at the end of each year on that portion of the interest earned during the year.

MONEY MARKET MUTUAL FUNDS These short-term savings accounts are available from mutual fund companies. *Pro:* They pay higher interest than bank accounts and CDs, plus you can write a few checks per month on them. *Con:* They aren't insured, and the minimum investment may be higher than a bank would require. *Taxes:* Like other dividends, income is taxed at ordinary income tax rates during the year it is earned.

STOCKS These investments buy ownership in publicly traded companies. *Pro:* As a company becomes more profitable, their stock price usually rises. The company may pay dividends, too. *Con:* Stock prices go down as well as up, and dividends aren't guaranteed. *Taxes:* Stock investments cause tax hits in two ways. First, since dividends are quarterly or annual payments, they get taxed just like interest—at ordinary income tax rates. Second, when you sell stock and its value has gone up, you pay taxes on the increase, called a *capital gains tax*. Alternatively, if the stock's value declines between the time you buy and sell, you'll get a tax deduction for the loss, called a *capital loss*.

BONDS These are contracts companies or governments make with you to pay interest for the use of your money over a period of time, usually a number of years. *Pro:* Bond prices tend to be more stable than stock prices, and interest is often higher than stock dividends. *Con:* Prices seldom appreciate as much as stocks. *Taxes:* Bonds pay interest that's taxed as income, just like the interest on your bank accounts. There are, however, a few twists. For example, interest on tax-free municipal bonds is not taxed federally, and some bonds are also free from state and/or local taxes.

MUTUAL FUNDS You buy shares in an account that pools your money with money from other investors to buy a variety of stocks and/or bonds. *Pro:* A professional picks investments on your behalf, for relatively little cost. *Con:* Performance and fees vary widely from fund to fund. *Taxes:* Most mutual funds pay dividends. Like other dividends, they're taxed at ordinary income tax rates during the year they are earned. You will be responsible for the taxes on the gains regardless of whether you reinvest or not. If you sell your shares in a fund, capital gains rules apply, as if it were a stock.

CAPITAL GAINS AND LOSSES

Capital—it's an old-fashioned word for invested money. A capital gain is the money you earn on investments, while a capital loss is the money you lose. Uncle Sam wants a piece of whatever you earn, but at a lower tax rate than ordinary income tax. If it's a **short-term gain** (money made on an investment held less than one year) you will be taxed at your ordinary tax rate. If it's a **long-term gain** (money made on an investment held more than one year) you will be taxed 20 percent if you are in the 27 percent bracket or higher. (If you are in a lower tax bracket, your tax is 10 percent.) If your investments go sour, you can deduct the loss against any capital gains and up to $3,000 per year against any other income.

individual *retirement* accounts

Investments that give you a tax advantage

THINK OF YOUR IRA AS A CONTAINER that can hold stocks, bonds, mutual funds, CDs, and other investments. What's unique about IRAs is that they let you defer paying taxes on those investments until you reach retirement age, which in IRA-land is 59½. The idea is that by that age your income will be less and you will be in a lower tax bracket than in your prime working years. Ergo, the taxes you now have to pay on your IRA investments will be less.

The U.S. government set up different types of IRAs to allow people to save for retirement. Chances are you have one or two IRAs lying around. Now it's time to sort through the paperwork and figure out what you've got.

INDIVIDUAL RETIREMENT ACCOUNTS (IRAs) Up until your retirement, you've probably been putting money into an IRA. If you earned less than $42,000 a year while single or $62,000 combined while married, then you had a **deductible IRA**. This means that you were allowed to contribute between $2,000 and $3,000 per year and deduct that contribution from your income. Now, when you are ready to withdraw, you will pay taxes on what you contributed as well as what you earned, presumably at a lower tax rate.

If you made more than that, you could still have contributed to an IRA, but the money you contributed would not have been tax-deductible. Hence its name—**nondeductible IRA**. That said, all the money your investment earned got to grow, tax free. So when you are ready to withdraw your money, you pay taxes only on what you earned, not what you contributed.

ROTH IRAs This type of IRA allows people who earned up to $110,000 if single, $160,000 combined if married, to contribute up to $3,000 a year after taxes to a Roth IRA. The really good news is that "qualified withdrawals" from your Roth IRA are tax free as long as your account has been open for at least five years.

ASK THE EXPERTS

How do I know whether my IRA is a traditional deductible or a nondeductible IRA?

You were allowed to contribute to two kinds of IRAs. In the first kind, the annual contributions would appear on your old tax returns as deductions. In the second type of IRA account, the contributions consisted of money you had paid income tax on. Any of these contributions should have appeared on form 8606 of your tax return for the year you contributed. It's important to dig out this information—since you won't have to pay taxes again on that money when you withdraw it, only on the earnings from it.

Aren't there sometimes penalties on withdrawals from IRAs?

Yes. If you're under 59½, you'll owe an additional 10 percent penalty on the amount withdrawn, as well as the regular income taxes—unless you become disabled. Then you pay only the ordinary income tax. You may also be able to get an exemption from the penalty for medical expenses that are above 7.5 percent of your gross income, payment of health insurance premiums if you are unemployed, and certain first-time homebuyer expenses. Talk to your accountant about how to proceed.

IRAs: distributions and taxes

Once begun, annual distribution must continue

OH, HAPPY DAY, YOU FINALLY get to start withdrawing money from your IRA just like you planned. The IRS lets you start taking money out of your IRAs once you reach 59½. If you prefer, you can wait until you are 70½ before you withdraw a dime. These withdrawals are called **required minimum distributions** or **RMDs**. But watch out: If you don't start taking distributions by then, the penalty for "excess accumulation" is—take a deep breath—50 percent of the amount you should have taken. Clearly, the government wants you to withdraw all of the money from your IRA during your lifetime—and pay tax on income that was deferred, or face serious consequences.

In most cases, the money you put into the account was never taxed. And over the years, your IRA investments have been earning interest, dividends, and capital gains that were also never taxed. Now it's time to pay up. The good news is that since you are no longer working, you will probably be in a lower income tax bracket and so will pay less money in taxes on your IRA withdrawals.

Once you turn 70½, how do you know how much to withdraw each year? The amount you're required to take out is determined by a formula: Every year you look at your IRA's ending balance from the prior year and divide it by a factor based on the average life expectancy of a person your age, which the IRS has figured out for you. Look in the *Uniform Lifetime Table*, found in IRS Publication 590. (Get a copy of it by calling 800-829-3676, or download it from **www.irs.gov**. It's a good idea to check since the tables are periodically updated.) The amount of taxes you pay on your RMD will depend on two factors: your tax bracket and whether your IRA was deductible or nondeductible.

NOW WHERE DO I GO?!

How do I go about beginning the withdrawal process for my IRAs?

If you have reached the magic age of 59½, you can begin withdrawing money from your IRA. To do this, simply contact the bank, mutual fund company, or brokerage house that holds your IRA account. If you are 70½, you must start this process or face stiff penalties.

If I have more than one IRA, do I have to take distributions from each?

You should calculate your RMD for each IRA separately. However, the IRS lets you add up all of your RMDs and take the total from one or more IRA(s) of your choice, as long as the total amount withdrawn is correct.

What happens to my IRA if I die before the age of 59½?

Funds in the IRA pass to your heirs without the penalty. However, they will have to pay income tax on the distribution. Whether estate taxes are owed depends on the size of your whole estate (see page 170).

FIRST PERSON   DISASTER STORY

Beneficiary Blues

My dad's IRA was in the same bank where he had been a customer for 50 years. When he died after taking minimum distributions for 10 years, his accountant told me that there was more than $100,000 left in the IRA, and that I was probably the beneficiary. When I called the bank, they said there was no beneficiary form on file for Dad's account. It must have gotten lost over the years. My accountant says that many institutions lose these forms, especially if there have been mergers or if the institution is too small to have a separate pension department. Since there is no beneficiary, the IRA becomes part of Dad's estate and all the money from the IRA has to be paid out and taxed over the next five years. Had Dad given me a copy of his IRA beneficiary form when he filled it out, I could have delayed the bulk of the taxes until I retired.

—Sherry Z., Abilene, Texas

roth IRAs

It offers unique investment advantages if you plan to continue working

IN 1997 A NEW KIND OF IRA WAS BORN: the Roth IRA. Although you don't get a tax deduction on your contribution, it was an instant hit, because it has some advantages that are especially suitable to retirees:

● Income and capital gains earned are not just tax deferred, they're tax free. In other words, the Roth allows its owner to avoid taxes on whatever he earns. (Regular IRAs start taxing you when you take out money.)

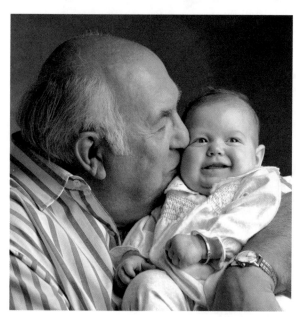

● Uncle Sam doesn't make you take out Roth money if you don't need to, so it can continue to grow tax free. (The feds require annual minimum distributions from regular IRAs.)

● Allowances for distributions before you turn 59½ are more lenient for Roths than for regular IRAs. For example, if you're a first-time home buyer, you can take out money tax free, as long as your Roth is at least five years old. If you need money for certain college or medical costs before you turn 59½, you can withdraw Roth earnings penalty free, but you'll owe taxes on the earnings.

● As long as you're still working and have earned income, you can still contribute to a Roth account, regardless of your age. (You can't contribute to a regular IRA after you turn 70½.)

The bottom line? If you have a Roth IRA, you'll want to spend it last, since 1) it continues to earn tax-free money; 2) it has few distribution restrictions; and 3) it can be left to your heirs.

ASK THE EXPERTS

When can I start taking distributions of earnings from my Roth IRA?

When you turn 59½, as long as you've met the five-year "holding period requirement," you can take out as much as you want, tax free. (The clock starts once you make your first Roth IRA contribution.) But if you need the money before five years have passed, you'll generally owe tax on any withdrawals beyond your contributions.

If I'm taking minimum distributions from my regular IRA, but don't need the money, can I contribute them to my Roth IRA?

No. You can only contribute income you've earned from work.

I understand that I can "convert" my regular IRA to a Roth IRA. How?

You may convert part or all of your regular IRA to a Roth as long as your modified adjusted gross income is less than $100,000, excluding the amount of the Roth conversion. When you do this, you're essentially taking money out of your regular IRA, getting taxed on it, and then putting it into a Roth. While you would owe taxes now (on the amount converted), your future earnings and distributions would be tax free as long as you hold the part you converted for at least five years.

Is converting to a Roth IRA and paying the taxes on the amount converted a good idea when I am retiring?

Every situation is different; check with a professional adviser before making this decision. If you need to spend your IRA during retirement, then you won't mind taking the required minimum distributions of a regular IRA. Tax rates need to be considered, too. For example, if you're in a high tax bracket just before you retire but will be in a lower one after you retire, converting before you retire would mean that the amount you convert is taxed at a higher rate, so you might wait. But a Roth conversion might be smart if you won't need the funds during retirement. Since there is no minimum distribution you have to take from a Roth, the money will grow, tax free, during your lifetime; then it'll pass to your heirs.

annuities

Reliable income is the prime attraction

WHAT IS AN ANNUITY? Well, it's a cross between an IRA and a life insurance policy. Like IRAs, annuities allow you to invest in a variety of assets (stocks, bonds, mutual funds), and the earnings on those investments are tax deferred. And just like IRAs, you can start to take your annuity payments as early as age 59½, but like life insurance, there's no limit on the amount of annuity you can buy, and payments you receive are linked to actuarial tables.

During their working years, most people buy either a **single premium deferred annuity** or a **variable annuity**. Single Premium Annuities pay a fixed rate of return on the money you deposit. Variable Annuities are a little spicier since they are invested in one or more mutual funds and pay a potentially higher rate of return, but can also be more volatile.

Now that you are retiring, you may want to consider an **immediate annuity**. Here you buy an immediate annuity in one lump sum and then decide to take payments over a fixed period of time or over your lifetime. If you choose the lifetime payment option, your monthly payment will depend on your current age, your sex, and whether or not payments will continue to be paid to your spouse or the beneficiary when you die.

ASK THE EXPERTS

I'm scared that I'll run out of money. Should I buy an immediate annuity to make sure I'll receive payments for life?

It depends. The amount that the insurance company pays you is based on the assumption that you'll live to a certain age. If you die before that time, the insurance company will get to keep the rest of the payments. On the other hand, if you're healthy and have a family history of longevity, an immediate annuity might pay off for you. You could have a chance of outliving the insurance company's projection and coming out with even more payments than they had planned to give you.

My financial adviser is trying to talk me out of buying an annuity. He says bonds would be better. Why is that?

Most studies comparing annuities with other investments show that returns on annuities usually fall short after expenses and taxes are taken out. Remember, you pay 20 percent tax on a capital gain. So unless you're in a very high tax bracket and money has been socked away in the annuity for a long time, an annuity may not be a good idea. It's true, immediate annuities can give you peace of mind by providing guaranteed income each month. However, the high costs and low payouts make comparison shopping essential. For a steady rate of return you may find you'd be better off investing in bonds or other fixed-income assets instead.

I bought a variable annuity 15 years ago, and now I want to tap into it. How do I do that?

You have several choices. Choosing to "annuitize" essentially converts your variable annuity into an immediate annuity. While lifetime income is good in theory, few people actually make this choice. Why? The amount paid out is usually small, and the payments end with your death—even if the payments just began! If you want a continuous stream of income, consider going with fixed payments. And if you just need a one-time withdrawal, lump-sum options are available. If you die while you're taking fixed payments or a lump-sum payment, your beneficiaries are still entitled to receive any original contributions that haven't been taken.

now what do I do?

Answers to common questions

I'm trying to decide whether to tap into my IRA or my other investments to cover some living expenses. Any suggestions?

It depends on your tax situation and the size of your nest egg. Withdrawing from your non-IRA assets first is usually best. This is especially true if you're in a high tax bracket, since part of your withdrawals from non-IRA assets may be taxed at the lower capital gains rates instead of ordinary tax rates. If, however, you're in a low income tax bracket and you have a large IRA, you might want to start withdrawing money from your IRA before you need it. Why? As long as your withdrawals don't put you into a higher income tax bracket, you'll be able to draw on this account with low tax consequences. Finally, if you have a Roth IRA, this should be tapped last. If this sounds confusing, ask your tax adviser to help you understand the pros and cons of each choice.

I've always had a rainy day fund. Where should I invest it now that savings account rates seem so low?

Money Market Mutual Funds are the ideal investment for boosting your returns without significantly increasing your risk. These funds are available from your favorite mutual fund company, and they generally allow you to write a few checks a month, should you need this money.

I hear tax-free bonds are a good investment. Would they be right for my IRA?

No, tax-free bonds have no place in an IRA or a Roth IRA. Retirement plans such as these are already tax deferred or tax free, so a tax-free bond would give you no advantage whatsoever. The same is true even in your regular portfolio if you're not in a high income tax bracket. The taxes you save must be sizable enough to make up for the lower rate of return that a tax-free bond pays.

I'm thinking about shifting all of my investments from stocks to bonds in order to generate more cash each month. Is this a good idea?

Not if you want your retirement money to last for a long time. While a total shift to bonds will boost your current income, over time inflation will eat away at your portfolio, and you'll be forced to deplete your savings. Instead, don't be afraid to maintain some stock exposure to offset inflation.

Aren't there sometimes penalties on early withdrawals from IRAs?

Yes. If you're under 59½ and withdraw any money, you'll owe a 10 percent penalty on the amount withdrawn, as well as the regular income taxes. If you become disabled and withdraw the money, you pay only the ordinary income tax. You may also be able to get an exemption from the penalty for medical expenses that are above 7.5 percent of your adjusted gross income, or if you're unemployed and you need the money to pay health insurance premiums.

OW WHERE DO I GO?!

WEB ADDRESSES	PUBLICATIONS
www.invest-faq.com Comprehensive, unbiased introduction and reference to investing.	**You're Fifty—Now What?: Investing for the Second Half of Your Life** by Charles P. Schwab
www.troweprice.com **www.vanguard.com** These mutual fund companies provide a wide range of educational services on their sites.	**The Complete Idiot's Guide to Buying Insurance and Annuities** by Brian H. Brevel
www.mpowercafe.com A good source of information for retirement planning.	**Financial Fitness for Life** by Jerry Mason

insurance needs

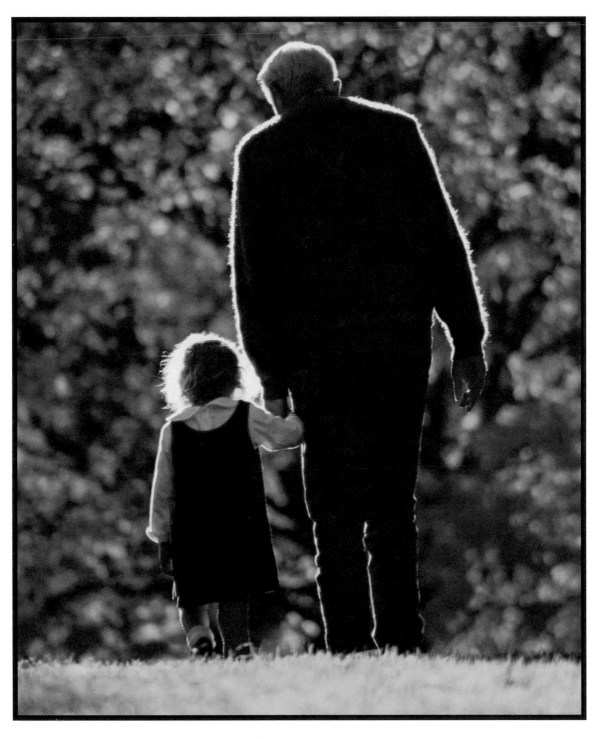

Are long-term care insurance premiums tax deductible?

life insurance

You may not need this coverage anymore

BY NOW, YOU MUST KNOW THIS BIT of financial advice by heart: Life insurance buys you peace of mind because your loved ones are protected financially when you die. But along comes retirement, and guess what? Your situation may not require as much life insurance as when you were working. After all, it's likely that you no longer have to protect your dependents (they're out on their own), or your spouse (the mortgage may be paid for and child care is just a memory).

If no one is relying on you for financial support anymore, it's time to check to see if other retirement income, such as your pension, will support your spouse after your death. Consider this:

- **IF YOU HAVE WHOLE-LIFE OR "PERMANENT" INSURANCE:** First, decide if the money you are spending on **premiums** (the amount you pay each year for the insurance) could be invested more wisely. Find out how much money you'd get if you cashed out now; this is called **cash value**. It's based on the insurance company's investment of the premiums you've paid up to this point (less administrative costs and the cost of the insurance itself). Then look at the opposite page to evaluate how you might put that money to use.

- **IF YOU HAVE TERM INSURANCE:** Many people buy a policy with the term expiring at retirement age. If the term's not up on your policy, and you don't need the coverage anymore, you can just cancel it. (Unlike a whole-life policy, term insurance doesn't have a "cash value" that you can retrieve.) But if the premiums are relatively low (usually they're not), you may want to hold on to the policy.

- **IF YOU HAVE A GROUP LIFE POLICY AT WORK (USUALLY TERM LIFE):** Ask your employer what happens to that policy when you retire. In some cases, the insurance ends promptly; in others, it may be phased out over a period of years with the company paying part or all of the premiums. If it ends, and you need to extend your coverage for any reason, you may be able to convert your employer's group coverage to an individual policy at a reasonable cost.

ASK THE EXPERTS

I have a whole-life insurance policy with a face value of $100,000, and the cash value at present is $50,000; I'm 67 and just retired. All my financial ducks are in order, and I feel I don't need this insurance coverage anymore. What should I do?

If you need income for retirement, cash out the policy. Take the money, plus what you've been spending on premiums, and invest it (see page 16). If you won't need the income, spend that money on your grandchildren or a dream vacation.

What if I need to preserve coverage to care for my wife, who is 15 years my junior, but I want to lower or eliminate the need to pay premiums?

You have several options:

- You can change your whole-life policy to *extended term* insurance. This way you stop paying premiums and use the cash value that has already built up in the policy to buy a term policy (paid in full, so no premiums) with the same face value as the original whole-life policy. The difference: The extended term policy is only good for a limited number of years.
- You can change your whole-life policy to *lifetime term* insurance. Like the extended term, you stop paying premiums and use the cash value to buy a paid-up term policy. But instead of being a policy for a limited time period, it's for life. The difference? When you die, lifetime term will pay less than an extended term policy.
- You might be able to reduce the face value of the policy. (Not all insurers will do this, but it won't hurt to ask.) You'll still pay premiums, but they'll be half the original amount.

(see page 16)

TAKE CARE OF THE LAST RITES

You and your spouse might want to buy two small lifetime term insurance policies, one for each of you, to cover your funeral expenses and the costs of settling your estates. The amount should be $5,000 to $10,000, depending on your area and the size of your estate; ask your lawyer how much would cover everything.

medicare

Medicare is low-cost health insurance for people over 65

WHEN YOU TURN 65, YOU'RE ELIGIBLE for Medicare, the health insurance plan offered by the federal government. You pay no **premiums** (or fees) for part of this coverage (Part A), and you pay very low premiums for the rest of it (Part B). In 2002, Part B cost $54 per month.

About 39 million Americans are currently covered by Medicare. Unlike Medicaid (with which it is often confused), Medicare coverage is not based on need. That means it doesn't matter if you're rich or poor. You're eligible for Medicare if you are 65 and you and/or your spouse have paid Medicare taxes at work for at least 10 years. (You can find out for sure by calling the Social Security Administration, 800-772-1213.)

PART A is hospital insurance. If you go into the hospital, you pay a deductible (the bills you pay for before the insurance starts to pay anything) and a portion of the costs; Medicare picks up the rest:

DAYS IN HOSPITAL	YOU PAY
0–60	$812 worth of bills
61–90	$203 per day
91–150	$406 per day

Medicare also pays a portion of your outpatient bills and covers short-term home health care and hospice care.

PART B is medical insurance. After you pay a deductible ($100 in 2002), Medicare covers 80 percent of the amount designated as appropriate for most doctors' fees, and for medical equipment and supplies (wheelchairs, pacemakers, etc.), and other services such as mammograms and X-rays that Part A doesn't cover. A few selected costs are covered at 100 percent.

ASK THE EXPERTS

What health services are not covered by Medicare?

Some of the services and supplies that Medicare does not cover—under Parts A or B—include the following:

- most prescription drugs
- routine physical exams
- dental care
- routine foot care, such as corn or callus removal
- custodial care, such as assistance with bathing, eating, and dressing
- eyeglasses
- hearing aids
- dentures
- orthopedic shoes
- health care received while traveling outside the U.S.

(See page 132 to learn how to get coverage for these conditions.)

What is meant by the term "Medicare + Choice"?

That term can be misleading. Medicare + Choice is just a name that Congress used broadly, in 1997, to include all Medicare-related options, such as managed care Medicare plans. The term doesn't mean that the basic Medicare program has changed.

HOW DO I GET MEDICARE COVERAGE?

You're automatically enrolled in Medicare the month you turn 65 if you already get Social Security benefits. If you are close to age 65—and not getting Social Security—you can apply for both Medicare and Social Security at the same time. You will receive a packet in the mail containing your Medicare card and instruction booklets. There will also be some forms to sign and return by mail. When you sign the forms, you'll be asked if you want Part B, which is optional. If you opt for Part B, the premiums are usually deducted from your monthly Social Security checks. (If you don't want to start your Social Security at 65, you will get a monthly bill for Part B premiums instead.) If you have questions, call 800-772-1213.

medigap insurance policies

A medigap policy picks up the slack in the Medicare program

IF MEDICARE DOESN'T PAY FOR A DEDUCTIBLE or part of your doctor's fees or for prescription drugs or dental work or podiatrists, who does? Good question—you do. Fortunately, to offset such costs, you can buy a medigap policy. It's a supplemental insurance policy sold by private insurance companies. As its name implies, it fills the gaps for many services that aren't covered by Medicare.

There are 10 standard medigap plans to choose from, starting with the most basic (and cheapest) plan, A, and ending with the most comprehensive plan, J. The letter designations are required by law so that retirees can easily compare and evaluate the policies. Each of the policies offers various additional benefits. Plans H, I, and J, for instance, cover prescription drugs. Not all plans are available in all states, but in Minnesota, Wisconsin, and Massachusetts, you'll have even more choices. (See opposite page for chart outlining benefits for each plan.)

When shopping for a medigap policy, consider the services you need and the price. Plans F and J generally cost less, for example, because they have a high deductible. (You'll have to pay $1,580 out of pocket per year before this plan kicks in a dime.) All standardized medigap plans are also sold as Medicare "Select" Plans, which usually cost less because you must use certain doctors and hospitals (except in an emergency).

WHO SELLS MEDIGAP MANAGED CARE PLANS?

Contact your state insurance commissioner or the state Department for Aging to find out which insurance companies sell them in your area.

Although the benefits offered are standardized according to the letter designation on each plan, the cost of premiums is not. Premiums for the same plan can vary from one insurer to the next. You will want to shop around for the features you need at the cost you can afford.

THE STANDARD MEDIGAP PLANS

All companies offering medigap insurance must offer Plan A, consisting of basic benefits (below). They may also choose to offer any (or all) of Plans B–J.

THE BASIC BENEFITS

HOSPITALIZATION: The plan pays coinsurance for hospital days covered by Medicare Part A.

MEDICAL EXPENSES: The plan pays coinsurance for Medicare Part B (generally 20 percent of Medicare-approved expenses) after the $100 deductible is met.

BLOOD: The plan pays for the first three pints of blood used each year.

Coverage in Each Type of Plan	A	B	C	D	E	F*	G	H	I	J*
Basic Benefits	✔	✔	✔	✔	✔	✔	✔	✔	✔	✔
Part A: Inpatient Hospital Deductible		✔	✔	✔	✔	✔	✔	✔	✔	✔
Part A: Skilled-Nursing Facility Coinsurance			✔	✔	✔	✔	✔	✔	✔	✔
Part B: Deductible			✔			✔				✔
Foreign Travel Emergency			✔	✔	✔	✔	✔	✔	✔	✔
At-Home Recovery				✔			✔		✔	✔
Part B: Excess Charges						100%	80%		100%	100%
Preventive Care					✔				✔	
Prescription Drugs								Basic Coverage ✔	Basic Coverage ✔	Extended Coverage ✔

*Plans F and J also have a high deductible option. If you choose this option, you must pay **$1,580** out of pocket per year before the plans pay anything. Insurance policies with a high deductible option generally cost less than those with lower deductibles. Your out-of-pocket costs for services may be higher.

different types of *healthcare* plans

Insurance for early retirees

IF YOU RETIRE EARLY AND ARE NOT OLD ENOUGH for Medicare, there are three basic types of health insurance to consider getting:

FEE-FOR-SERVICE PLAN Also known as a traditional indemnity plan, it offers the most flexibility. You choose your own doctors and hospitals, and you can visit a specialist without getting approval from your regular doctor. The premiums are the most expensive. Also, you may pay an annual deductible of $500 to $1,500 before the insurance company starts paying your bills, and they usually pay just 80 percent of the "reasonable and customary" (average) medical fees; you're expected to pay the remaining 20 percent of that average plus any overage between what the doctor charges and the average fee. You often must pay bills up front and wait to be reimbursed by your insurance provider.

PREFERRED-PROVIDER OR POINT-OF-SERVICE PLAN You choose your primary care physician from a list of doctors who have agreed to accept fees proposed by the insurance company. Your primary care physician often must approve any other health care you receive. This insurance policy costs less than fee-for-service, and the co-payments (fees you pay for medical services) are likely to be lower. Some plans provide options for seeing doctors or going to hospitals not listed in their plan if you pay a higher percentage of the fees.

HEALTH MAINTENANCE ORGANIZATION, OR HMO This plan assigns your care to a doctor within its group (often housed together in a clinic). All other healthcare is subject to that doctor's approval and is performed only by specialists and hospitals within, or designated by, the HMO. The fees you pay for medical services are nominal, but if you see physicians or seek hospital care outside the HMO, you'll pay the costs in full.

WHEN YOU TURN 65, MEDICARE OFFERS OPTIONS SIMILAR TO THOSE FOUND IN THE PRIVATE SECTOR:

"Managed Care" Medicare Plan

The basic Medicare plan is a traditional fee-for-service plan. You choose your doctor and hospital; Medicare pays for submitted bills. But in recent years, Medicare recipients have been able to join managed care plans such as preferred-provider plans and Health Maintenance Organizations (HMOs) just like other insured individuals. These plans may offer the same benefits that you receive under the original Medicare plan, plus coverage of some of the gaps in Medicare. You pay a monthly premium to the managed care plan, and sometimes you pay minimal co-payments for services. Before picking a managed care plan, however, be sure you understand exactly what is covered and what the costs are.

A Medicare "managed care" plan is not a medigap policy. Rather, it's a different way of delivering Medicare benefits, plus it also covers many Medicare gaps and some services Medicare does not cover at all. Generally, these managed care plans are cheaper than medigap plans (even the "Select" variety) and offer more choices. You can pick from an HMO with a point-of-service option or a preferred-provider option.

Medicare "Select" Plan

Medicare "Select" is an HMO-type of medigap plan available in some states. The insurer offers a choice of some of the standardized medigap coverages A through J— to be used in conjunction with your basic Medicare coverage. However, the "Select" policy generally costs less than other medigap policies because you must use specific hospitals and in some cases specific doctors to get full insurance benefits (except in an emergency).

paying for *health* insurance

Medical coverage from your former employer is best

IF YOU RETIRE EARLY, THAT'S ANY time before age 65, you won't yet be eligible for Medicare. You need to think about your health insurance: Who's going to provide it? How much will it cost? And how far ahead will you have to purchase a new plan to cover preexisting conditions—health problems that you've had for a while, such as asthma or diabetes? Don't worry. You have some options:

YOUR FORMER EMPLOYER'S HEALTH PLAN If your company offers continuing health coverage after early retirement, great; go for it. Check any changes in the coverage, though. For example, the deductible may change for retirees, or fewer services may be covered. You may pay a monthly premium (the fee for insurance coverage) that's higher than the premium you paid while working.

COBRA/HIPAA If your employer doesn't offer early retirement medical insurance, you can buy it under the Consolidated Omnibus Budget Reconciliation Act (COBRA). Thanks to this Federal law, you are guaranteed the right to buy 10 months' coverage—individual or family—through your former employer's group plan. Benefits must be identical, but you'll pay the full premium (and it's usually pretty hefty). After 10 months, the insurance company is required by the federal Health Insurance Portability and Accountability Act (HIPAA) to extend your coverage, regardless of preexisting conditions, but they may raise the rate. COBRA coverage is often cheaper than buying an individual policy on your own, and the follow-on policy, while even more expensive, may be worth it until you're eligible for Medicare.

AN INDIVIDUAL POLICY It's often the most expensive option because premiums are based on your age and medical history. Ask about coverage for preexisting conditions. Some insurers wait up to a year before they pay bills related to these conditions (in which case you will need to overlap such a policy with your COBRA coverage—an added expense). A few companies won't cover services related to preexisting conditions at all; avoid them.

TOP SIX COBRA FACTS

- You're covered under this law if your company employs 20 or more workers and offers its employees group health insurance.
- Your spouse and dependent children are also eligible for COBRA, sometimes for as long as three years.
- COBRA does not apply to federal employees, some church-affiliated organizations, or companies that employ fewer than 20 workers. It is also not available in the District of Columbia.
- To be eligible, you must have been covered under a former employer's health plan.
- Individual health insurance policies that you buy yourself are not subject to COBRA law.
- You must be offered identical plans (medical, hospitalization, dental, vision), but you have the option of dropping noncore benefits (dental or vision) if you don't want to pay for those.

FIRST PERSON   DISASTER STORY

Worth the Money at Any Price

My husband and I had been planning his retirement for years. We were thrilled when Harry's company offered him an early retirement package at 62, except there were no medical benefits. "Don't worry, Ethel," he said. "We'll have Medicare at 65, and I'll buy a policy to tide us over till then." Well, after his COBRA coverage ran out, the cost of extending the policy was going to be really expensive. So we decided to go without insurance until Medicare kicked in. But within a year, Harry had a really bad bout of pneumonia. He managed to stay out of the hospital, but just barely. Now we're sweating it out, hoping we make it to 65 before either of us has a medical emergency. We should have bought that insurance when we could. You just can't take chances with your health.

—Ethel S., Manchester, New Hampshire

long-term care
insurance

The costs of long-term care can wipe out a lifetime of saving

WAIT, DON'T TURN THIS PAGE. This is really important. The need for long-term care is rising—especially since so many of us are living longer, thanks to those good doctors. But while the doctors are brilliant at dealing with many acute problems—a heart attack, surgery for a broken hip—they can't do much for chronic conditions that require long-term care, such as a stroke, Alzheimer's, or Parkinson's.

This type of care—dubbed **long-term care** by the insurance industry— ranges from the skilled nursing services that you'd receive at a nursing home to the custodial care you'd receive in your own home if you needed help with the "activities of daily living." The costs for such services can be steep. One year in a nursing home can range from $30,000 to $100,000, depending on the state you live in and the facility you go to. Bringing an aide into your home for three three-hour visits per week to assist with bathing and dressing can run about $1,000 a month or more, again depending on the area in which you live. Yet costs for such care on a long-term basis are not covered by traditional health insurance.

That's right: *not covered*. Not by Medicare. Not by medigap policies. (Medigap plans D, G, I, and J do contain an at-home recovery benefit, but it's only for short-term assistance). Long-term care is not even covered by private health insurance or your employer's health insurance, or by any of the traditional forms of insurance that you've always relied on.

Yet almost half of America's elderly citizens will require some type of long-term care. To protect yourself, you need a separate, long-term care insurance policy. Offered by life insurance companies, these policies vary widely in terms of eligibility requirements, restrictions, costs, and benefits. (See page 141.)

ASK THE EXPERTS

I'm in good health. Why should I get long-term care insurance?

None of us think that we're going to be the ones to get sick—especially if we've always enjoyed fairly good health. But the odds of entering a nursing home—and staying for longer periods—increase with age. By the year 2005, it's estimated that nine million men and women over the age of 65 will need long-term care. One study, in fact, shows that 40 percent of people aged 65 and older will enter a nursing home. About 10 percent of those folks will stay there five years or longer.

But doesn't Medicare cover nursing home care?

Medicare will cover just 100 days of nursing home care, and only when it follows a hospital stay. And that's it. If you must stay longer (the average stay is two years), you'll be expected to pay the bill yourself.

If I need long-term care and I don't have a long-term care policy, who will pay for this care?

You will, until your money runs out. Once you've exhausted every bit of your investments and savings and met federal poverty guidelines for income and assets, you will be eligible for Medicaid. (Your spouse would be able to retain your home and a very small income.) Medicaid will pay the nursing home expenses for you indefinitely, but the nursing home you are in must be one that accepts Medicaid patients.

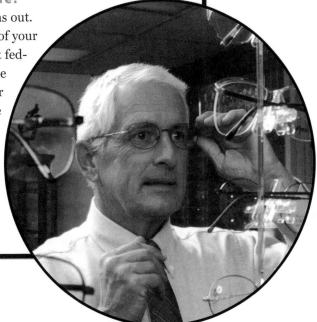

buying
long-term care
insurance

GREAT. YOU ACTUALLY READ ABOUT long-term care insurance. Now, do you need to buy some? It's not necessarily for everyone. According to the National Association of Insurance Commissioners:

You should not buy long-term care insurance if:
- You have limited assets; for example, you don't own a home.
- You don't have heirs whom you want to inherit your assets.
- Your income is very low, say from Social Security benefits or Supplemental Security Income (SSI), so that you often have trouble paying for basic needs, such as food, medicine, housing, or utilities.

You should consider buying long-term care insurance if:
- You have significant assets and income that you want to pass along to your spouse or heirs.
- You want to pay for your own care independent of Medicaid or support from others.
- You want to protect your spouse from a drop in income should you need long-term nursing home care.

Here's how the pricing works: Like most other types of insurance, the younger you are when you buy the policy, the cheaper your premiums will be. Prices for long-term care insurance climb sharply once you hit age 65. It would have cost about $650 per year if you had bought a policy at age 45 that pays $100 a day for three years' care. At 65, that same policy will cost you about $1,550 per year.

Obviously, a good time to buy a policy is when you're a bit younger, say between the ages of 50 and 55, before the prices skyrocket and/or your health declines. In addition to rising costs, the other problem with waiting to buy a long-term care policy, of course, is that minor health problems can develop and may require you to pay a higher premium. The good news is, the premiums on long-term care policies may be tax deductible; check with your accountant. Many insurance companies offer long-term care policies. Look for a company that has been providing long-term care coverage for at least 10 years.

FEATURES TO CHECK OUT IN A LONG-TERM CARE POLICY

Daily benefit A policy that pays $100 per day will cost less than a policy that pays $200 per day.

Deductible (elimination period) A policy that starts paying after 100 days will cost less than one that starts paying after 20 days.

Services covered Will the policy cover in-home care? Under what conditions? Find out what services are excluded.

Waiver of premium This feature lets you stop paying premiums while you are receiving benefits.

Inflation protection Your benefits may be adjusted for inflation, but your premium remains the same.

Renewability Most polices are guaranteed renewable. That means the insurer can't cancel your policy even if you develop a terminal illness. However, they may raise your premiums.

State of residence Nursing home costs vary from state to state. Check with several nursing homes in your area and ask about their cost per day.

Where can I get long-term care insurance?
Contact the National Council on Aging at 202-479-1200 for more information on long-term care insurance. A number of life insurance companies offer it. Contact: John Hancock, **www.johnhancock.com**, 800-695-7389; Continental Western Group, **www.cwgins.com**, 800-235-2942; Fidelity National Financial, Inc., **www.fnf.com**, 888-934-3354; Mass Mutual, **www.massmutual.com**, 888-229-7540.

IF YOU'RE RESISTING

You're in good company. Because long-term care insurance is so expensive, many advisers counsel retirees who could afford three years in a home (about $100,000 in many states) not to buy it. Or they suggest that you simply invest the money you might pay for long-term care insurance in a special account. Chances are, by the time you need a nursing home, the account will be large enough to take care of the bills. And if you never need it, the money is available for your heirs. Granted, there's a risk, since you could get sick before the account is big enough to cover long-term care expenses. But that is a risk many people feel comfortable enough to take.

medicaid

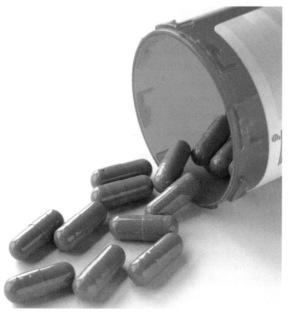

MEDICAID. MEDICARE. THESE NAMES SOUND so much alike that it's no wonder people often confuse them. They are both national health insurance programs, but they are *not* interchangeable.

- Medicare is a health insurance program for people age 65 or older. (You may also qualify for Medicare if you're a younger person with a disability or with chronic kidney disease.)
- Medicaid is a health insurance program for low-income people of any age. You can be young, old, or in-between to qualify for Medicaid.

Only if your money runs out—all of it— will Medicaid pay your long-term care bills

Medicaid is a federal program, but it is administered by the states. That means the rules for eligibility and coverage can vary from one state to the next. State regulations even affect how you apply for Medicaid; in one state you go through your local county social services office, in another you go to the welfare office, and in another you must find the Department of Human Services office.

If you qualify for Medicaid and are over 65, it's possible that you'll receive coverage from both Medicare and Medicaid. Medicaid, for instance, can pay your Medicare deductible, your Medicare Part B premium, and that 20 percent of charges not paid by Medicare. In many states, Medicaid also covers services and costs that Medicare does not cover, such as prescription drugs, eyeglasses, and nursing home care, although you might have to pay a small amount for certain services.

Ask THE EXPERTS

What long-term care services does Medicaid pay for?

It covers costs for an extended nursing home stay and/or assisted living at home. If you or your spouse needs such care (called "custodial care," because it does not require major medical services), and you don't have long-term care insurance to cover the charges (see page 138), you'll have to tap into your personal savings to pay the bills. Only when your money runs out does Medicaid kick in.

What is this "spend down" business all about?

To qualify for Medicaid as the insurance of "last resort," you must have spent everything you have. Whether you wind up on Medicaid or rely on it from the start, the drawback is the same: You must generally exhaust all of your assets and money before Medicaid will help you. The regulations shift slightly from time to time, but currently you must have no more than your home and furnishings, a car, a burial plot, and money for burial expenses to go on Medicaid, and your spouse also must have few assets and little income.

Are all nursing homes required to accept Medicaid?

The most desirable nursing homes often don't accept Medicaid patients at all, since Medicaid usually doesn't pay the full amount they charge. Some that have a few designated Medicaid beds will take you as a nursing home resident paying the full fees, then hope to switch you to a Medicaid bed when you run out of money. But if there is no Medicaid bed available at the time you need it, there is a slight chance that they will just ask you to leave. Transferring to a nursing home that accepts Medicaid can be a problem at that point. If nursing home care is recommended for you or your spouse, it is wise to get advice from a social worker or a lawyer who specializes in elder care in your area.

TRANSFERRING YOUR ASSETS

If you want to transfer your assets to your heirs, hoping to fall back on Medicaid if you should need long-term care, check out your plans with a lawyer specializing in elder care so you can avoid any difficulties. The feds are allowed to examine the last three years of your financial transactions at the time you apply for Medicaid. If a transfer was made to defraud the government and make it seem that you have no assets, you could be subjected to fines and even jail time.

now what do I do?
Answers to common questions

I'm thinking about tapping into my life insurance policy to have a little extra spending money. What are the financial consequences?

It depends. If you borrow against the policy, you'll be charged interest, and the amount your heirs receive will be reduced accordingly. If you cash in your policy, you'll get taxed on any earnings that might have built up while you owned it, and you'll reduce your coverage. See pages 128–129 for more on cashing in your life insurance.

What's not covered in a long-term care policy?

Limitations and exclusions will differ from policy to policy. But in general, long-term care policies often don't cover mental and nervous disorders such as depression and schizophrenia, alcoholism and drug abuse, and self-inflicted injuries. If, when you buy the plan, you have preexisting health problems that will lead to long-term care, such as Alzheimer's or Parkinson's disease, they won't be covered either.

Are long-term care policy premiums tax deductible?

Yes, but it isn't simple. First, you must itemize deductions. Next, the amount you can deduct depends on your age, the top limit being $2,570 at age 70. Finally, you must add the premiums to your other medical premiums and expenses for the year and determine how much exceeds 7.5 percent of your adjusted gross income. For example, if your adjusted gross income for the year is $50,000, you can only deduct medical expenses that exceed $3,750. If all your medical expenses and premiums for the year add up to $4,000, you will only be able to deduct $250.

I've heard that there's a financial advantage to buying medigap insurance soon after going onto Medicare. How does that work?

If you buy within six months of enrolling in Medicare Part B, you cannot be turned down or charged extra due to any preexisting health condition. After that, an insurance company can charge extra if you are in poor health or even refuse to sell you a policy. (Some states have different rules; check your state insurance agency.)

Do I need collision or comprehensive insurance on my old car?

No. If your car is at least five years old, an insurer won't pay much for it. You should only insure items that you can't afford to replace. (The same goes for extending appliance warranties.)

Now that I'm retired, do I still need disability insurance?

No. In fact, you can't buy such a policy even if you want it. Disability insurance replaces income, so you can't buy a policy unless you're earning a salary. (Investment income doesn't count.) Even if you're taking care of your wheelchair-bound spouse around the clock, you can't buy a disability policy unless you're receiving an income.

Is there a lot of paperwork involved in submitting Medicare claims?

Medical providers are required to submit your bills to Medicare for payment, so you do not have to bother with that paperwork. Once Medicare pays, the providers send you bills for the amount Medicare doesn't cover. It's a good idea to get a copy of all the bills your doctor is sending to Medicare.

NOW WHERE DO I GO?!

WEB ADDRESSES	PUBLICATIONS
www.insure.com This consumer insurance site helps you research insurance issues and find answers to your insurance questions.	**The Complete Idiot's Guide to Buying Insurance and Annuities** by Brian H. Brevel
www.acli.org Consumer-oriented site for the American Council of Life Insurance, a trade group. Helpful info on life insurance and long-term care insurance.	**Life and Health Insurance** by Kenneth Black and Harold D. Skipper, Jr.
www.medicare.gov or 800-633-4227 This federal government site offers answers to frequently asked questions about Medicare, Medicaid, and medigap policies. The site also has a link called Medicare Compare that connects you with Medicare managed care plans.	**Medicare and You 2001** by the Health Care Financing Administration

elder *abuse*

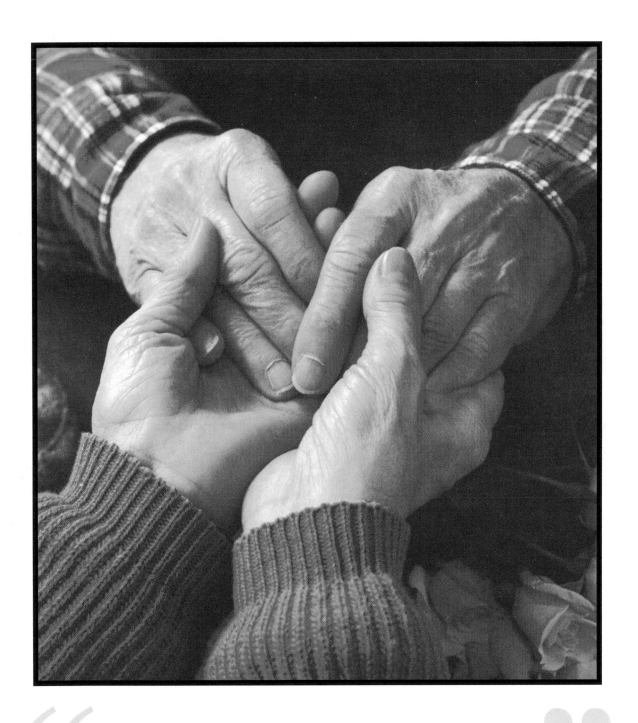

"*The many physical and emotional vulnerabilities that come with aging can make seniors prime candidates for abusers.*"

a hidden *epidemic*

Protect loved ones now—and yourself later on

ELDER ABUSE ISN'T EPIDEMIC AMONG THE POOR and uneducated; it's an equal-opportunity misery that can affect anyone. In the last year, more than 550,000 older adults were reported abused or neglected in the U.S., but the actual incidence may be four to five times higher than what is reported. In most instances, caregivers, relatives, and advisors treat an older person with the respect and the dignity they deserve. However, the many physical and emotional vulnerabilities that come with aging can make seniors prime candidates for abusers.

While physical abuse is the most easily recognized form of elder abuse, exploitation can take many different forms. Financial abuse is the illegal or improper use of an older person's funds, property, or resources. Psychological abuse is the mental or emotional anguish caused by threats, humiliation, or other verbal or nonverbal behaviors. Domestic abuse is an escalating pattern of violence by an intimate partner in which the violence is used to exercise power and control. Sexual abuse includes any nonconsensual sexual contact with an older person. Neglect is the failure of a caregiver to fulfill his or her caregiving responsibilities.

The losses that come with abuse can be devastating. Life savings can disappear. Health can be compromised. Dignity and security are no longer taken for granted. So before someone you know becomes another statistic—or even worse, one of the unreported ones—make sure you are aware of what constitutes abuse and can recognize the signs. This will also be good to know for when you yourself are aged and in need of care.

THE CAUSES OF ELDER ABUSE

There is no clear-cut answer to the question of what triggers elder abuse, though there are some theories. According to the National Center on Elder Abuse, it's a very complex problem that involves the mental and physical states of both the victim and the abuser.

In the case of physical abuse, for example, this behavior can be a holdover from the abuser's younger years. For example, adult children who are financially or emotionally dependent on a parent because of their own drug abuse or personality dysfunction, may act out and become irresponsible caregivers.

Other theories of elder abuse include caregiver stress and burnout, or the inability to manage an older person, who may demonstrate disruptive behavior or suffer from dementia. The bottom line is that there is no excuse for abuse. It is a crime that it is punishable by law.

NOT JUST A NURSING HOME PROBLEM

Statistics from the National Center on Elder Abuse (NCEA) show only 10 percent of elderly people who need assistance live in a long-term care facility, such as a nursing home. The remaining 90 percent live either alone or with loved ones. So, abusers of elderly people can be anyone that the person depends on or comes into contact with. This can include family, neighbors, professional caregivers, friends, and landlords. For more information, visit the NCEA Web site at **www.elderabusecenter.org**.

money *matters*

Finances and the elderly

FINANCIAL ABUSE OF THE ELDERLY can be very difficult to spot. By the time visible signs, like dwindling assets or a stack of unpaid bills, become apparent, some form of financial exploitation has probably gone on for quite a while.

There is no one profile for an individual who will take advantage of a senior's finances. These people can be telemarketers, con artists, or even a son or daughter.

Despite the subtlety of many forms of financial abuse, there are some warning signs that point to a person who is being exploited by a relative or a professional financial adviser. According to AARP (American Association of Retired Persons) and other educational, advocacy, and resource groups, these warning signs include:

■ Sudden changes in bank activity, such as the withdrawal of large sums of money, as well as redirected bank statements or numerous canceled checks for "cash" to caregivers, advisers, or others.

■ New "roommates," such as previously unknown relatives or acquaintances, who move in with an older person and begin to assume financial responsibilities.

■ Power of attorney is suddenly changed to a new person, especially in instances where the older person is incapable of understanding the document or its ramifications.

■ Unexplained transfer of house title to a friend or acquaintance.

■ Unusually high fees for home improvement or routine maintenance.

■ Poor grooming or personal care provided to elders by caregivers, even though the caregivers are provided with the necessary funds to purchase items like food and clothing.

PREVENTING FINANCIAL ABUSE

For an older person, one of the most heart-wrenching forms of financial abuse is exploitation by a loved one. To protect yourself in the future—and to protect a loved senior right now—there are some simple steps you can take:

■ **Talk about finances** Discuss the estate plan and who will manage a loved one's money should the need arise. Obviously, this should be done sooner rather than later, when a loved one may be suffering from cognitive problems or physical ailments.

■ **Get it in writing** Treat all personal loans as a bank manager would. If a senior is lending money to a child or other relative, get a promissory note. Sure, that loan may be forgiven at some point, as specified in a will or at an executor's discretion, but it always makes sense to be as formal as possible when loaning money.

■ **Require fiduciary responsibility** The person who assumes power of attorney should give a regular accounting to all family members of monies spent or invested. You can have a clause written into the power of attorney documentation that specifies this request.

■ **Check up on the caregiver** Too often, family members allow a caregiver to assume all responsibility, leading to caregiver burnout and abuse of the elder or the elder's finances. Make both scheduled and unscheduled visits to check on things.

■ **Keep lists** Maintain updated records on anyone involved in an older person's financial transactions. That includes the gardener, home maintenance people, and the local bank teller(s). Check invoices to ensure an older person is not being overcharged for services.

■ **Keep a visual record** Taking pictures of a home's assets can help prevent problems in the future. If you notice something of financial or personal value is missing, you will have a visual record to prove its existence.

abuse by financial *advisers*

How to spot con artists and scams

THE FINANCIAL SERVICES INDUSTRY operates by a code of ethics, serving their clients' needs carefully by keeping a client's goals in mind when making recommendations. However, in any profession, there are always some unscrupulous characters whose goal it is to take advantage of the unsuspecting and the naïve.

Protecting yourself or a loved one against these folks requires vigilance. Even some upstanding investment advisers who began as honest purveyors of financial advice can go bad in a tough economy, leading them to mismanage others' money or, in the worst case, to take off with an investor's entire retirement savings.

Fortunately, you can prevent yourself or someone you know from becoming a victim by following these self-defense tips:

CHECK OUT STRANGERS AND "STRANGE" DEALS The Central Registration Depository of your state securities agency can provide extensive background information on investment salespeople and firms. Almost all investment opportunities must be registered in the state in which you live.

ALWAYS STAY IN CHARGE OF YOUR MONEY If you understand little about investments, take the time to educate yourself or involve a family member or a professional, such as your banker, before turning any money over to a stranger who promises great results.

MONITOR YOUR INVESTMENTS AND ASK QUESTIONS Too many older Americans not only trust unscrupulous investment professionals and outright con artists to make financial decisions for them, but

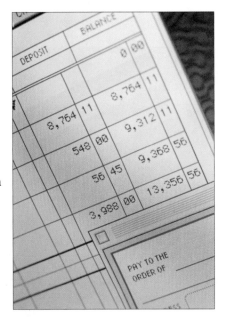

compound their errors by failing to keep an eye on the progress of their investments. Look for signs of excessive or unauthorized trading of your funds. Do not be swayed by assurances that such practices are routine or in your best interests. Do not permit a false sense of friendship or trust to keep you from demanding routine written or oral reports. When you suspect that something is amiss and get unsatisfactory explanations, call your state securities agency.

BE ON THE ALERT FOR PROBLEMS CASHING OUT If someone with whom you have invested stalls you when you want to pull out your principal or profits, you may be a victim of fraud. In many cases, investing advisers will pressure you to "roll over" nonexistent "profits" into new and even more alluring investments, thus further delaying the point at which the fraud will be uncovered.

BEWARE OF "RELOAD" SCAMS Most older Americans are dealing with a finite amount of money that is unlikely to be replenished in the event of fraud and abuse. The result is a panic well known to con artists, who have schemes for taking a "second bite" out of victimized seniors. Faced with a loss of funds, some senior citizens will go along with another scheme (allowing themselves to, in effect, be reloaded) in which the con artists promise falsely to make good on the original funds lost, and possibly even generate new returns beyond those originally promised.

emotional *abuse*

EMOTIONAL UPHEAVAL CAUSED BY INSULTS, threats, harassment, intimidation, and humiliation is another aspect of elder abuse, and it can be devastating to an older individual. Plus, it often escalates into other forms of abuse, especially physical violence.

The signs of emotional abuse can be subtle. For example, you may have listened to your golf partner's tirades for years, but only now do you notice that his ailing wife is really starting to look depressed. Or perhaps a sibling who acts as a caregiver for a parent is becoming increasingly short-tempered.

Look for the warning signs

It can be difficult to gauge how serious these scenarios are. But by staying alert, you may be able to stop an abusive situation before it gets out of hand. Warning signs of emotional abuse may include:

- Frequent emotional upset or agitation
- Fearful behavior, especially around certain individuals
- Withdrawal and apathy
- Unusual behavior such as sucking, biting, and rocking
- An elder's report of verbal abuse or mistreatment

Elders can also suffer from other, more insidious forms of emotional abuse that may be harder to spot. For example, a caregiver may isolate an elder from family or friends, or prevent that person from engaging in regular activities as a form of punishment—or simply out of spite. The best way to stay alert to this kind of abuse is to familiarize yourself with an elder's routine and be aware of any sudden changes. And stay in touch with the elder's emotional state and question any profound shifts.

ASK THE EXPERTS

I think my friend is emotionally abusing her mother. The last few times I have been over there, he wouldn't let her come out of her room. What should I do?

First, you need to understand that what may seem like emotional abuse to you may be a fairly benign, generally nonabusive aspect of caring for an older individual. For example, if your friend is talking loudly and sounds exasperated, perhaps his mother is hard of hearing and refuses to wear a hearing aid. If, however, you are noticing behavioral changes in your friend that stem from caregiving issues, or think that your friend's mother is becoming increasingly withdrawn or forced into isolation, then it is time to intervene. Talk to your friend about what's going on in his life. Suggest that he discuss things with someone skilled in caregiver support or join a support group for caregivers.

I often hear my neighbor yelling at his elderly, wheelchair-bound uncle. I've tried getting him to stop, but nothing's changed. Is this abuse?

While this is a prime situation in which abuse can develop, this could also be a serious example of caregiver stress. Your neighbor may have other problems making it hard for him to provide adequate care for his uncle. However, if talking to him has not seemed to help, then consider reporting this to your county area Agency on Aging (**www.n4a.org**; 202-296-8130) or your state's Department of Aging. Their number should be in your phone book. This agency keeps all reports of suspected abuse confidential. You could be providing an invaluable service to your neighbor, and to his uncle.

physical and sexual *abuse*

So many cases go unreported

Many people expect the elderly to injure easily, so they may not be alarmed by unusual bumps and bruises. Unfortunately, however, those bumps and bruises may be signs of physical or even sexual abuse.

Physical and sexual abuse can take many forms, some more overt:

■ Food or water may be withheld as punishment, resulting in malnutrition or dehydration. Look for sudden weight loss and cracked lips.

■ An open wound or sore, especially in those who have no other health problems, can be a sign of abuse. Look for bruises or welts around the wrists or ankles, which can indicate use of improper restraints.

■ Patchy hair loss can be a sign that someone is pulling the elder's hair.

■ Overmedicating to keep an older person quiet or undermedicating as a form of punishment or extortion are also forms of abuse. Watch for changes in prescriptions or in an elder's mood or level of alertness.

Because these signs are often not noticed—even by trained professionals—many cases go unreported. Elders themselves may be loath to report abuse because they may be afraid to lose the caregiver (despite the misery the caregiver inflicts) and put into a nursing home. Or, like younger people in abuse situations, they may feel they deserve the punishment or abuse because they are a "burden" to a caregiver. Or victims may be too cognitively impaired to recognize that they are being abused.

The most common perpetrators of this kind of abuse are family members or caregivers. Concerned relatives, friends, and neighbors may not report suspected abuse out of fear of being wrong and causing embarrassment or further problems. Don't be afraid to discuss concerns, or report them to the county area Agency on Aging so they can investigate.

Signs and symptoms of sexual abuse include but are not limited to:

- An elder's report of being sexually assaulted or raped
- Bruises around the breasts or genital area
- Unexplained venereal disease or genital infections
- Unexplained vaginal or anal bleeding
- Torn, stained, or bloody underclothing

The typical elderly victim of physical or sexual abuse is:

- Female
- 75 years old or older
- Widowed/divorced
- Lives alone or with the abuser

- Dependent on the abuser
- Physically or mentally impaired
- Frail or chronically ill
- Isolated from friends and relatives

FIRST PERSON   **SUCCESS STORY**

Rude Awakening

It's hard to watch your parents get old, and even harder to accept it when their faculties start to go. After Mom died, Dad's dementia got so bad that we had to hire a caregiver to be with him 24/7. Someone in my office recommended a caregiver she knew. All was fine at first, but then I started noticing Dad was getting bedsores. He never complained about them, but I was worried, so I started paying surprise visits to the house. Every time I dropped by I found the caregiver watching TV or talking on the phone. Then it dawned on me that the caregiver was leaving my father in bed for days at a time without turning him or adjusting his position. I fired the caregiver, filed a report on her, and hired a registered nursing service. Within weeks, the terrible bedsores were gone.

—Paulette M., Sheridan, Mississippi

neglect by
caregivers

Spotting benign and intentional neglect

ONE OF THE HARDEST THINGS TO DETERMINE when it comes to elder abuse by caregivers is if it's intentional or accidental. Either way, an elder's life may be at stake. Whether the caregiver is a professional or a relative, and works in the elder's home or in a nursing home, he or she has the same responsibilities.

When a caregiver withholds attention from an elderly person and fails to meet that person's basic needs, it is considered neglect. And neglect is a form of abuse, whether it's intentional or accidental.

Neglect by caregivers can include:

- Withholding or not providing adequate food and water
- Withholding clean clothing or aids such as canes or reading glasses
- Creating unsanitary or dangerous living conditions
- Withholding medication
- Failing to meet the elder's daily needs or personal hygiene needs
- Failing to manage the elder's money, if the caregiver has responsibility for paying bills, or failing to manage the budget for caring for the elder person

To stay alert for signs of neglect, it may help to require documentation by caregivers of any accidents or lapses in normal care. A good caregiver will immediately let you know if a fall occurred and how it occurred.

Another way to monitor and improve the care of an elder is to have all care requirements spelled out in writing. Be as specific as possible, and give a copy to the caregiver and her agency. Make sure to include relevant emergency numbers.

<aside>
BE ALERT!

An older person, especially one who is isolated or lives alone, may also suffer from self-neglect. This is often the result of chronic illness, depression, or financial problems, or from the elder's unwillingness to ask for help.
</aside>

FINDING THE RIGHT NURSING HOME

Many people think that the best way to prevent elder self-neglect is to put an elderly person into a nursing home. It usually is, but neglect happens in nursing homes, too. Be vigilant about the facility you choose for an elderly person. Here are some tips for picking a safe place:

■ Ask for opinions. Consult your family doctor, friends, local clergy, and area Agency on Aging to get opinions regarding nursing homes in your areas. You can even talk to current residents to get their opinions.

■ Contact your state long-term care ombudsman, whose job it is to resolve conflicts and to work to improve the quality of nursing-home care within your state. The ombudsman may be able to provide inspection reports. In addition, ask the nursing-home administrator for the contact information of the home's assigned ombudsman.

■ Make unannounced visits. Visit the nursing home on weekends or evenings, when the staff-to-resident ratio is likely to be the lowest and services may be reduced. See how the nursing home handles these off-hours.

■ Take the elder with you to visit facilities you are considering. See how he or she reacts to the facility, its services, and its residents.

■ Use the Web to investigate. But be wary about any information you find on the Web, especially when it comes to a facility that touts its own services. Verify all information independently. The federal government and Medicare allow you to compare nursing homes at **www.medicare.gov/Nursing/Overview.asp**. Or visit the American Association of Homes and Services for the Aging (**www2.aahsa.org**).

now what do I do?

Answers to common questions

I am so worried that my elderly neighbor is suffering from self-neglect. He has no family. What can I do?

First, learn the facts about elder abuse and neglect—that's the best way to help friends or family members. All older people should have some type of regular contact with family, friends, or neighbors. Especially if the elder is housebound, frequent visits will improve the elder's quality of life. Even something as simple as a daily telephone call will help you monitor the well-being of an older person. If you can do that for your neighbor, that would do much to help. What also might help is seeing if you can encourage him to develop a social support network, say by joining the local seniors' association in town. Another option is to contact programs such as Meals on Wheels (**www.owaa.org**; 703-548-5558) or church groups, which will pay visits to elderly people, providing meals and much-needed social support.

How is elder abuse prosecuted?

Acts of violence—including assault, battery, theft or rape—are crimes in every state, no matter how old the victim is. And depending on the particular consequences for the victim, certain emotional abuse and neglect cases are also subject to criminal prosecution. Plus, according to the National Center on Elder Abuse, most states have laws that address elder abuse and levy harsher penalties on those who victimize older adults. Many state attorney generals' and district attorneys' offices have set up specialized elder abuse investigation and prosecution units. In addition, communities nationwide are creating special units of law enforcement and adult protective services or are electing ombudsmen to investigate elder abuse cases. Even financial abuse is getting a closer look: specialized FBI teams and insurance claims detectives are increasingly investigating financial fraud cases.

I am pretty certain my elderly aunt is being abused by my uncle, but I am afraid to report him. If I can get her to go to the doctor, will the doctor report it?

Doctors and professional caregivers, such as home health providers, are obligated to report suspected cases of abuse or neglect. However, we are all responsible. Experts at the National Center on Elder Abuse advise anyone who suspects abuse or thinks an elder is in a life-threatening situation to call the police immediately. That makes sense, but the harder thing to do is to report suspected abuse that doesn't seem life threatening. Don't be afraid to speak up—you could be saving a life. Adult protective care services, your state ombudsman, and your local area Agency on Aging are all good places to start. All calls are confidential.

OW WHERE DO I GO?!

WEB ADDRESSES	PUBLICATIONS
www.elderabusecenter.org The National Center on Elder Abuse	**Ending Elder Abuse: A Family Guide** by Diane S. Sandell and Lois Hudson
www.aarp.org AARP (American Association of Retired Persons)	**Crime and Elder Abuse: An Integrated Perspective** by Brian K. Payne
www.aoa.dhhs.gov/abuse/default.htm Administration On Aging—Elder Abuse	**Getting Older, Getting Fleeced: The National Shame of Financial Elder Abuse and How to Avoid It** by Pamela Camille
www.consumerlaw.org National Consumer Law Center	**The Caregivers' Roller Coaster: A Practical Guide to Caregiving for the Frail Elderly** by Billie Jackson
www.consumerlaw.org/initiatives/seniors_ initiative/telemarketing_fraud.shtml Consumer Facts for Older Americans: What to do if you've become the victim of telemarketing fraud	

CHAPTER TEN

internet

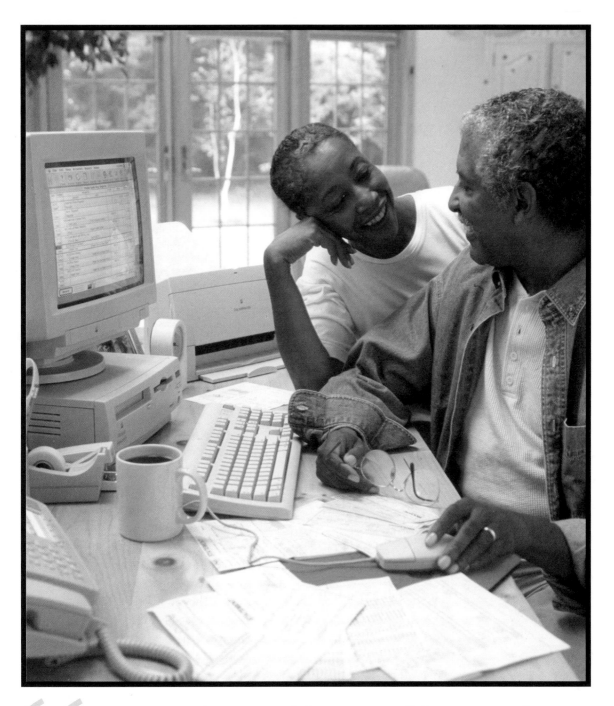

Imagine being able to send letters, photos, videos over the phone! What a world that would be. Well, ahem, it's here.

what is the *internet?*

What is it, and why should I care?

SO WHAT EXACTLY IS THE INTERNET? Well, it's best explained by its nickname, the Information Superhighway. It's like a huge highway that wraps around the entire world, with zillions of connecting byways, main streets, even dirt tracks. Instead of cars and trucks, little packets of computer information are going along the paths carrying pictures, programs, text, and sounds from anywhere in the world to your computer. Like a real road system, the Internet gets occasional traffic jams, but usually you can go another way.

How do you get onto this highway? You need an **Internet Service Provider** (sometimes called an ISP; more on those on pages 170–171), which provides an on-ramp for your computer. Once you're online, you can use an electronic mail program to exchange messages and use a program called a **Web browser** to visit **Web pages**. These pages contain text and pictures. And Web pages also contain **links** to other Web pages. These links are often underlined in blue text; click on a link (more on these later) and you'll find yourself, ta-da, on another Web page. It's these links that gave rise to the Web's name—if you imagine all the links in all the pages as lines, you'd have a mass of threads as intricate as a spiderweb.

ASK THE EXPERTS

How did the Internet come about?

Back in the 1960s two trends that seem unrelated gave birth to the Information Superhighway we know today. A few universities across the United States had just developed **supercomputers** (computers that can process huge amounts of data quickly), and the academic world wanted to share their research and computing power. So the supercomputer centers **networked,** or linked up, with each other and allowed other, less powerful, computers to access them. Meanwhile, the U.S. Department of Defense wanted to create a channel of communication that could withstand heavy bombing and still be able to carry military intelligence back and forth. So they developed a network too. When the two networks were connected, they became the Internet. Since then millions and millions of smaller networks have joined in, and things have never been the same.

Is the Internet the same thing as the Web?

No, it's not. The Internet is like a network of roads that carries information. The biggest use of the Internet continues to be delivering pieces of electronic mail (e-mail). The World Wide Web also uses the Internet roadway, but instead of simple mail messages, it lets you stop and explore (i.e., browse) the sights in graphic detail, for example, photos of things for sale at online stores, news videos, and audio clips.

Who invented the Internet?

It's hard to give the credit to one person or organization, because so many people were involved. The U.S. Department of Defense takes some credit—they put up the cash to create a network that would work even if bombs were dropped on a lot of communications lines. Vinton Cerf, a Stanford University researcher, came up with the rules of the road (the Internet protocols) that let different computers exchange information, which earned him the honorary title of Father of the Internet. And a physicist called Tim Berners-Lee came up with the idea (and name) of the World Wide Web.

getting
connected

What a modem does and why you need one

IMAGINE BEING ABLE TO SEND LETTERS, photos, videos over the phone! What a world that would be. Well, ahem, it's here. But instead of using your phone, you use your personal computer. Almost every computer you can buy these days contains a piece of internal hardware called a **modem** that's designed to plug into your phone wall outlet. You use it to dial up your Internet service provider and bring the Internet into your home.

All you need to get online is a bit of phone wire long enough to reach from the wall socket to the back of your computer. Plug one end into the wall socket and the other into the modem port. You'll see there are two ports (computerspeak for openings, or sockets). Make sure you don't use the one that's labeled with a stencil of a telephone (that's for a separate phone line if you want). Once your modem is tapped into the phone system, you are set to go online (connect up to the Internet). Whenever you are online, your phone line is in use, so you can't make or receive phone calls. Once you're done with the Internet, you can use the phone again.

When your modem is ready to roll, you're all set to hook up with a service provider. But first, you need to know how fast your modem runs. Most modems these days are rated at 56,000 bits per second (sometimes called 56K). Some older ones top out at 33,600 bits per second. When you select a dial-up number with your service provider, these numbers will be important. If you just bought a new computer, assume that its modem runs at 56K. Before you make the final jump onto the Internet, consider two much faster ways to get online. One uses your TV cable line to transfer Internet information, and the other uses a souped-up phone line. Computer folks call these faster connections **broadband.** Think of them as wide multilane highways compared to the narrow "dirt track" of a 56K modem connection. In fact, these connections are quite a bit faster—cable Internet can top 1.5 million bits per second. That's more than 25 times as fast as a regular 56K connection.

ASK THE EXPERTS

What should I do if I want to get calls while I'm online?

You'll have to have another phone line installed that you can reserve just for the Internet. Or you can connect up via your cable company or via a newer phone technology called DSL.

I've heard that my cable company gives Internet access. What gives?

It's true. Many cable companies can give you fast access to the Internet with a so-called broadband connection. This can be up to 25 times faster than dialing up using a modem, and it doesn't tie up your phone line. But there are some steps you need to know about.

1. You must plug your computer into a special cable modem, a boxy thing about the size of this book but twice as thick. The cable guy will bring this when he sets you up.

2. This cable modem must plug into a **network card** in your computer (also called an Ethernet card). If you don't have one, the cable guy may be able to fix you up.

3. Someone must program your computer's settings so it can communicate through the network card and cable modem to the service provider. Don't panic! The cable company will take care of this!

Network Card

going *online*

*Learn
about the
new phone
companies
of the
Internet*

TO USE YOUR TELEPHONE, you need the phone company to provide you with phone service. The same goes for your modem. But instead of the phone company connecting you, you need to sign up with a company that will provide Internet service—either an **Internet Service Provider** (or ISP) or an **online service** (America Online, Earthlink, CompuServe, and The Microsoft Network are some of the main ones).

What is Internet service? Well, it basically gives you access via your phone line to a big Internet computer that is linked to other Internet computers all over the world. Both an ISP and an online service will give you the telephone number of a computer near you that your modem can dial into to provide access to the Internet. (You want your computer to dial a local number so you won't have to pay long-distance charges each time you go online.) Some providers charge a flat monthly fee, while others charge by the hour. Part of this service includes an e-mail account. (See Chapter 11.)

Regardless of the type of service you choose, you will need to come up with two important things: your user name and password. A user name can be your last name or a made-up name. To protect your Internet privacy, we suggest you use a made-up user name, perhaps a nickname or your initials. Just make sure you won't mind giving it out as your e-mail address. Your password can be any word or set of numbers that you can remember easily.

ASK THE EXPERTS

Can someone eavesdrop on me while I'm online?

The risk of someone tracing where you surf online or reading what you write in chat rooms is pretty remote. For this to happen, a secret program has to be hidden in a suspect Web site—the kind run by shady characters. This is one of the many reasons why you should not visit Web sites listed in e-mail messages from people you don't know.

If I get an Internet account, can someone get into my computer files without my knowing it?

Any unauthorized entry into someone else's computer files is called **hacking** and is a federal offense. Hackers are usually not interested in private computers; they are after security holes in big Web sites. You can reduce the tiny risk of getting "hacked" by not staying online for long stretches at a time, say overnight.

Can I get a computer virus from the Internet?

Yes, computer viruses do abound online. A **virus** is a nuisance program that can infect software programs or files on your hard drive. They can cause your computer to crash (stop working unexpectedly) or they can come with a "payload" that could do anything from making it impossible to save files to erasing all the files on your hard drive! To protect your computer from viruses, most PCs come with antivirus software that starts up when you start your Windows software and runs constantly, ready to intercept any virus that comes on the scene. To be safe, don't open e-mail attachments from people you don't know or trust, especially if the attachment is a software program. If your computer didn't come with an antivirus program, you can buy software at most computer stores that detects and eliminates viruses. Be sure to go to the antivirus company's Web site often to get the latest, newest virus protection.

using an *ISP*

Going local has its advantages

YOU'VE PROBABLY SEEN ADVERTISEMENTS in your local paper exclaiming how you can connect to the Internet—just call one of these numbers and find out how. The phone numbers listed are Internet Service Providers, or ISPs. These are businesses that supply Internet access to people like you and me as well as to businesses. Many ISPs are local mom-and-pop operations, but some are large national or international corporations.

To find a local ISP, check your phone book under Internet Services. (If you don't see any listed in your region, then you'll need to use an online service. See page 172.) Check out the various benefits and prices of the ISPs in your area. For example, some bill you by the month, others by the year.

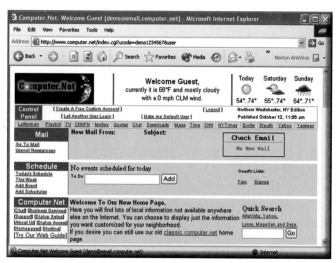

Most local ISPs offer local news on their welcome page. This ISP, Computer.Net in Westchester County, New York, also gives the weather.

Once you've chosen your ISP, it will give you the following information so you can get started:

- First, its Internet phone number, which your computer's modem will dial into (that is called an **access phone number**). Remember to make sure this is a local number.

- Next, you will be given the Internet "address" for the ISP's computer, which is called a **domain name server** address, or DNS (usually four sets of numbers, like 070.013.205.204).

- Finally, you will give the ISP your **user name** and **password**, so think about these before you call.

Ⓢ TEP BY STEP:

SETTING UP YOUR ACCOUNT

1. CLICK ON START, All Programs, then Accessories, then Communications, then New Connection Wizard.

2. IN NEW CONNECTION WIZARD CLICK ON THE NEXT BUTTON. Make sure Connect to the Internet is selected and press Next again.

3. THERE ARE THREE OPTIONS TO CHOOSE FROM: Pick an ISP from an existing list; set up a connection manually, or install the CD-ROM you got from an ISP. Pick whichever works best for you, then click Next.

4. DEPENDING ON YOUR CHOICE, follow the prompts until you are done. You may need to have handy the name of your ISP server, its phone number, and your user name and password.

5. WHEN DONE, click the Finish button

FIRST PERSON DISASTER STORY

Online/Offline

All I wanted to do on my computer was be able to get online so I could check out the action on some of these auction sites. I am a collector of wines, and more and more wine auctions are being held online. So I dialed up a local provider that my neighbor uses and got connected. Got all the information. Typed it all in. The DSN number, the ISP phone number, my number. You name it. When I was finished I restarted my computer, ready to start wheeling and dealing at one of the biggest wine auctions that afternoon. Nothing. Couldn't get online. Kept getting a message saying insufficient connection, try again. I kept trying and trying. I called the ISP provider and asked them what to do. We went over everything. All the numbers I had typed in were correct. So I tried again. And again. Still nothing. Needless to say, I missed the auction. Later that night, I called my ISP again to tell them to cancel my account, when they asked if I had added the number one in front of my area code and phone number. Yes, of course. "Oh, that's the problem. You don't need the number one." Oh. Swell.

—Sam R., Madison, Wisconsin

using *online* services

The Internet simplified

SO YOU THINK YOU WANT to go the online services route. It's a good way to get started using the Internet without getting too technical. Plus, many computers come with online service software already installed or at least some type of installation setup, so you're almost there.

Windows XP makes it easy to subscribe to an online service. Turn on your computer and modem and connect the modem phone line to your telephone wall jack. Click Start, All Programs, Online Services, and click on the service that you want to set up. Follow the steps and answer the questions as you go (clicking the Next button to continue through the setup).

Most likely you will be signing up for a new account. If you have any problems setting up your online service or finding an access number (which is the number your modem calls to get online), there should be some technical support numbers that you can call for help. Click the Help button on the opening screen and click through the contents to find the Member Support phone numbers.

ASK THE EXPERTS

I just got a CD in the mail from an online service promoting their software. How does that work?

The CD is basically a mini-trial of how the online service works. All you need is a phone line and a modem, and you're in business. You're getting a free trial without setting up an account. The free trial gives you a certain number of minutes "free" online to research, send e-mail—whatever you want.

I live in a rural area. Is there online service for me?

The chances of finding a local service provider are probably small. You can always go with a big online service. Just make sure it has a local phone number available in your area. If the closest number is a long-distance one, you will run up your phone bill by paying for long-distance connections or the extra fees often tacked on to utilize a toll-free number.

Which is better, an ISP or an online provider?

There are pros and cons to each one, many of which will change over time as online companies continue to improve their services. But for starters, ISPs are typically local outfits that can provide you with local service. That means anything from a home page that has local weather and movie information to easy access to a tech person to answer your tech questions. For some, local is nice; for others who work at 3 a.m. when the tech person is sleeping, it's a problem. Online providers offer national service with a slew of tech people to help you. That said, they also can suffer from online congestion because so many customers are trying to get online at peak hours, say 7 to 10 p.m. Online providers offer easy, speedy access to national news as well as national sites. Good advice: Compare prices and services before you sign up. And remember, nothing is forever. You can cancel and switch to another provider if you're not happy.

getting around
the web

You gotta use a board to surf the 'Net

YOU'VE GOT A MODEM AND A SERVICE PROVIDER.
Now what? You need something called a **browser**. That's the computer name for software that allows you to navigate the Internet. Think of it as the surfboard that allows you to surf the Web. Happily, your computer most likely came with a browser installed; some brand names are Netscape Navigator and Microsoft's Internet Explorer. If yours doesn't have a browser, you will have to purchase browser software at your local computer store and install it.

Here's how to begin using your browser:

1. Click Start, Internet (the option near the top left) to open your browser. You may also have your browser's icon on the Desktop, which you must double-click to launch your browser.

2. When the application opens, click on the Connect button in the Dial-Up Connection box. Your modem will begin dialing and log you onto the Internet.

When your browser software opens, it will most likely open to its home page (the screen you see when you first access a Web site). It usually contains an index, search options, and connections to other Web pages. Take a look at that home page. Do you see text that is underlined? Text that is darker and underlined is called a **hyperlink** (or sometimes just link). If you click on the underlined text, it will automatically "link" you to a different page or perhaps another Web site. If you click on a link and want to go back to where you were, click on the Back button on the Web browser button bar (located at the top of your screen, beneath the browser title bar). Notice that after you have clicked on a link, it is a different color—letting you know you have been there before.

WHAT IF

You want to print out a Web page?

Click the Print button on the Web browser button bar. It is at the top far right of your screen.

Your Web page doesn't display right away, and you see a page that says it didn't come up properly?

Click the Refresh button on the Web browser button bar.

You want to click on a link, but not exit the current page?

Right-click on the link and choose Open in New Window. This will open a new window along with the previous one.

You don't have an Internet Service Provider but want to get to the Internet?

You can get help from some online services. Click on Start, then on Programs, then on Online Services. You will see a list of various online providers. Select one, and it will ask you for your phone number. Then dial a toll-free number and find the best local access number for you. It will then ask for your credit card number and officially sign you up.

researching
online

*Surfing the
Web is as
easy as
catching a
wave*

THE INTERNET CONTINUES TO GROW with more and more information each day, which is stored in an abundance of **databases** (computer files full of systematically arranged information). In order to find what you seek, there are companies out there that have created user-friendly **search engines**—programs that tap into these databases by using **keywords**, a word or words that define your subject. Some names of popular search engines are Yahoo!, Excite, AltaVista, and Google. (For a listing of search engines see page 187.)

Here's how search engines work: If you want to look up information on puppies, you would simply type the key word *puppies* in the Search box and click the Search button. You will then see a list of underlined links (from news articles about puppies to sites that sell puppy food) to choose from. Click on the particular link that interests you, and away you go. To avoid getting a slew of links, narrow your search. For example, type *puppy food* in the Search box instead of just *puppy*.

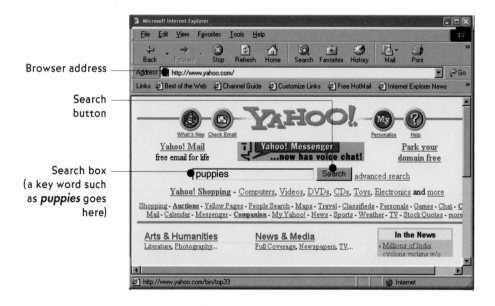

Browser address

Search button

Search box (a key word such as **puppies** goes here)

176

There's another way to search. You can go right to a specific site if you know its address. What is a **Web address**? It tells your computer where a company, an organization, even people (more on that later) are on the Web. Instead of using the Search box, you go up to the Address bar and type in the Web address and press Enter. You should immediately be taken to the home page of that address.

ASK THE EXPERTS

What do "http" and "www" stand for?

Get ready for a little technical lingo. HTTP stands for Hypertext Transfer Protocol. Basically, it's the code that allows you to send and receive stuff over the Web. You don't need to type in the http:// when you are browsing the Web. It will automatically do it for you. Most companies have "www" before their name, which stands for the World Wide Web. It's best to type it in the address field.

What are the slashes and dots doing in an Internet address?

The slashes and dots between words are providing specific location information about the address, a bit like a ZIP code.

How do I mark a Web site to come back to it again later?

Say you have found a new site that you really like. Instead of typing in its Web address every time, you can **bookmark**, or earmark, it for instant access. To bookmark a site, you must be currently looking at it. How do you bookmark? In Internet Explorer, go up to the Menu bar and choose Favorites, then Add to Favorites. The site's name will get added to your Favorites list. Next time you want that site, go up to Favorites and a list of all your added favorites will scroll down; click on your newly added site and it will instantly appear. In Netscape Navigator, you click on Bookmarks, then choose Add to Bookmarks. Next time you click on Bookmarks you'll see the name of your newly added site.

WEB ADDRESSES

A Web address is the address you type in to get to a place on the Internet. Nearly all Web addresses start with www for World Wide Web, then dot (typed as a period), then the name of the organization, then dot and an abbreviation. For instance, the Web address for Barnes & Noble is www.bn.com. For the Public Broadcasting System: www.PBS.org.
The last three letters of the address tell you something about the site:

.com a company
.org a nonprofit organization
.net a network provider
.edu school or university
.gov U.S. government
.mil the military

shopping
online

*No more
long lines
at the cash
register*

EVER GO SHOPPING AND FIND a parking spot right away, walk directly to the right department, and then discover that the item you are looking for is not there? Well, those days are gone. You can shop online, find what you want, and get it mailed to you; and if the vendors don't happen to have it, they'll mail it when they do. And chances are it will be cheaper than in the store, although there will usually be an extra charge for mailing it to you. All you need is access to the Internet, a browser, and a credit card.

Just as in the real world, there are a number of different ways to shop on the Internet: 1) directly from the manufacturer such as **www.ibm.com**; 2) from retail stores like **www.bn.com**; 3) from cyberspace-only stores like **www.eToys.com**; 4) from Internet malls like **shopping.yahoo.com**; 5) from online auctions like **www.ebay.com**; and 6) from catalogs like **www.landsend.com**. Some things never change: When you first get to a site you can expect to see specials, sales, and a pitch—just as you would at a local store.

How do you actually shop online? Well, most sites have you put your chosen items into a "shopping cart." A link then takes you to your checkout point—where you can review your merchandise, type in who you are and where you want your merchandise sent, and enter your credit card number. It will tell you the total cost including shipping and handling. Simply type in the appropriate information and your merchandise will be sent to you within the time that the "store" specifies.

Ask the Experts

How can I search for a particular item on a shopping site?

You can usually search for products by category, but it can be faster to use the site's search box. Type in the word(s) that describe the product, manufacturer, or type of goods, and click the Go button or Search button. Review the list of items and click on the appropriate link.

How safe is it to use my credit card online?

Don't type in your credit card number unless the site is **secure**, meaning that any information you give is **encrypted**, or coded, so that no intruder can use it. To determine if a site is secure, look for a closed padlock or unbroken key icon in the status bar along the bottom of the window. If the padlock is open, or the key is broken, the site is not secure.

Are my shopping habits ever kept track of?

Often when you buy things online, the seller puts a **cookie** into your virtual shopping cart. The cookie links your name to your purchase so the seller knows what types of goods and services you are interested in. (For more on cookies, see page 187).

GOOD DEALS BAD DEALS

Be wary. Just because it's online doesn't mean you are getting a deal. One thing in particular to watch for is the shipping and handling charges. You might find a site that has merchandise at a large discount, but by the time you add the shipping and handling charges, you would be paying more than you would if you went to the corner store.

auctions
online

Going . . . going . . . gone!

IMAGINE YOU'VE GOT A CLOSETFUL OF STUFF you don't use anymore. (Not too hard, is it?) Sure, you could hold a garage sale, but if you're tired of tire kickers trying to haggle you down, you can find a good home for more or less anything by holding an online auction. And once you've freed up space in that closet, you can bid on other people's unappreciated treasures to fill it up again!

Sure, dealing with strangers can be a leap of faith, but auction sites have a good self-policing system in place. Sellers and buyers build a reputation—people they do business with can leave electronic feedback about how friendly or fast a buyer or seller is. The more positive feedback you see, the more confident you can feel about doing business with someone. And if a deal goes bad, the auction site intervenes: Descriptions and bids are legally binding contracts. If there's any funny business, the auction site will usually revoke membership. Bad customers don't stick around long, so you can bid and sell with a fair amount of confidence.

There are a number of auction sites to choose from, and the list just keeps growing. For starters, you can check out **www.ebay.com** (shown here).

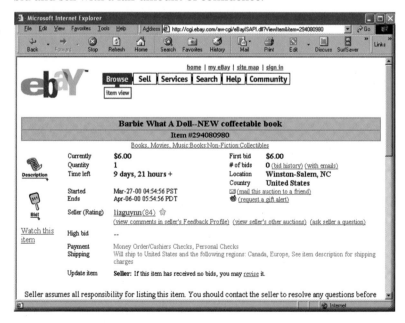

STEP BY STEP:

AUCTIONING

1. SIGN UP WITH AN ONLINE AUCTION SITE. Click on the site's Join link and be prepared to enter your real name, address, and e-mail address, as well as a screen name and password. If you're selling, you'll probably need to enter a credit card number or arrange to send a check to the company so that they can deduct an "insertion fee" (usually between a quarter and a dollar) for listing your item. They'll also want a percentage of the final bidding price—no more than 5 percent.

2. ONCE YOU'VE JOINED, you can put up items for sale. Sellers should set a realistic starting price (aim low to encourage bidders, but not so low that you'd be upset if you got only the opening bid). Compose an accurate description of the item (and be upfront about any faults or flaws—buyers don't like surprises). It's also helpful to find out before the auction how much it will cost to ship the item.

3. BUYERS CAN SEARCH FOR ITEMS by entering key words (Pokemon, Beanie baby, Chippendale chairs, and so on) in the site's Search box. The matching list is sorted by date, with the auctions about to close at the top. If an item seems interesting, click on it.

4. WHEN THE AUCTION CLOSES, the auction site will send e-mail to the highest bidder and the seller. These two must figure out the details by themselves in a fixed time frame—usually a week. They work out how to pay (check, money order, or whatever), how to deliver, and do what they've agreed on. Many sellers insist on waiting until an out-of-state check clears before delivering—so the buyer may wait a few weeks after the last bid before seeing the goods.

5. WHEN THE GOODS ARRIVE, it's helpful to leave a feedback message about the experience at the site. A good seller deserves praise, and other buyers deserve to know if a seller is slow or not very communicative.

chatting
online

Connect with people who have similar interests

EVER FEEL LIKE TALKING ABOUT YOUR FAVORITE hobby or local sports team, but there's no one around? If so, then Internet chat rooms may be just what you're looking for. It's a bit like instant mail. You type your comment, and someone responds. You can end up having a written conversation about everything from favorite soap operas to intergalactic space travel.

Online services have built-in chat rooms where you can talk about virtually anything with other people who share your service. If you have an ISP and are looking for a chat room using your Web browser, you can find a Chat link on most of the World Wide Web search engine sites (see page 187). You can also access these sites from your online service, but you need to use the Web link instead of your service's chat option.

You can choose many different topics to chat about in the free chat areas of **publicchat.msn. com**.

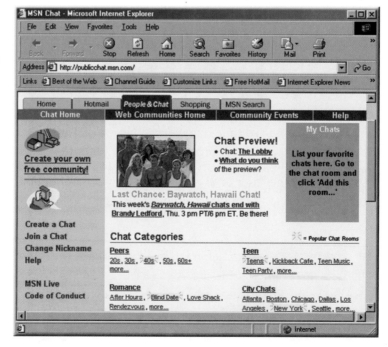

For an example of a typical online chat, try the free service available from The Microsoft Network.

1. Type **chat.msn.com** into the Address line, then press Enter.

2. Click the chat topic you are interested in.

3. Select a chat name (any nickname you fancy).

4. Click the connect button. You'll see chat software downloading into your Web browser window—don't panic! This is exactly what you need. When it's all installed, you'll be able to read chat messages in one chat window and type in your own comments in another. Your message is invisible until you click the Send button. Then it's posted for everyone to see.

5. To end your chat session, click the Exit This Chat button.

 **SK THE EXPERTS**

How do I send a message privately to one user?

You may invite someone (or they may invite you) to a private room if you are using an online service (or whisper with you—if you are using **http://chat.msn.com**), where you can talk one-on-one. To send a message to a particular user, highlight the user from the users list on the right, select the Private User option, and type your message (or type your message and click the Whisper button). Everything you type will be seen only by you and the other user until you turn the Private User option off (or stop clicking the Whisper button to send the message).

How do I screen out rude or annoying users?

To screen out obnoxious users, highlight the user from the users' list on the right and select the Ignore option.

how to *chat*

Just a few simple steps

WANT TO CHAT WITH SOMEONE ONLINE? Well, don't let the word "chat" confuse you—you'll be typing messages, not talking. And you'll both need to download and install a chat program and be online at the same time. But apart from that, it's all pretty easy. If you want to chat with people who use the America Online service as well as with people on the Internet at large, your best bet is to get America Online's Instant Messenger program, also known as AIM. Don't worry—it's free, and you don't need to subscribe to the company's online service to use it.

1. Go to **www.aol.com** to download the AIM program to your desktop. An icon of the AIM program will appear on your desktop. Double-click on it and it will open.

2. AIM will ask you to pick a screen name and password. The screen name you pick will appear on all the messages you type. Make a note of it and pass it around to your friends as your new AOL/AIM identification. And get their screen names too.

3. Every time you get online, AIM will start up and let your buddies know that you're available for a chat.

4. To see whether your buddies are online, add them to your "Buddy List"—all you need to know is their screen names. In AIM's Buddy List window, click on the List Setup tab and right-click on Buddies. Select Add Buddy and type in your buddy's screen name. Then click on the Online tab.

5. If your friend is online, you'll see his or her name in the Buddy List window. Double-click on it. A new window will appear. Type a quick greeting and press the Enter key.

6. When your friend sees you're starting a chat, he or she will send a reply. Don't be impatient—your friend may be away from the computer when you first say "hi." You can then hold a "conversation" by typing messages and hitting the Enter key to send them.

caroline - Instant Message

File   Edit   Insert   People   carolinelW's Warning Level: 0%

Hector: Got a minute?
Hector: What did you want to do for dinner?
caroline: I thought we could sacrifice one of the goats.
Hector: I was thinking more along the lines of Italian. I think there's a good one around the neighborhood somewhere

A A   A A A   B *I* U   link

Warn   Block   Add Buddy   Talk   Get Info   Send

now what do I do?

Answers to common questions

What does it mean when the computer says "Click here to download this file"?

Downloading is transferring a file; that is, copying it from the large group of computers that make up the Internet onto your computer's hard drive using your modem. You can download games, research information, or a program that will help your computer accomplish a specific task. Note that the larger the file, the longer it takes to download. So you have to have patience . . . or a really fast Internet connection.

Where can I get help getting online?

If you want help with getting connected to the Internet, click Start, Connect to, and you'll see a list of any Internet connections you have set up.

What do I do if I have call waiting on my regular phone line?

The call waiting signal will interrupt your Internet connection, which will most likely disconnect you. So before you go online, click on the Dialing Properties button in the Modem Properties dialogue box to disable your call waiting.

Where do I get help if my modem is giving me trouble?

Click Start, point to Help, type *modem* into the Help window keyword box, click the Display button, and then double-click on Troubleshooting Modems in the Suggested Topics list. Click the Click Here link to begin the troubleshooter. Click the circle(s) to the left of the description of your problem. It may take a while, but Windows will help you figure out what is wrong with your modem. It might not be your modem at all. It might be your individual online connection settings.

What does it mean when a message says "The page cannot be displayed"?

It could mean a couple of things. First, you might have typed in the Web address incorrectly; check it again to be sure. Second, the Web site might not exist, so you need to check the address that you are trying to type in. Third, if you received this message after clicking on a Web hyperlink, there might be something temporarily wrong with the site's Web server, so click the Refresh button on your Web browser and see if it works. If this doesn't work, simply try the link later.

Why do I sometimes get a busy signal when I try to connect to the Internet?

Most likely, your Internet Service Provider or online service has too many people trying to use it at the same time. This is similar to when you call a friend and their line is busy. It means someone is already using the phone line and you need to wait until someone hangs up. Just keep trying or try some of the different numbers your service gave you to dial in. If this is a persistent problem, contact your service and see how they can help you resolve this problem.

Do manufacturers get information about me from what I buy?

Yes. It's called a cookie. A cookie is a small file that some Web sites insert onto your hard drive when you visit them for the first time. The information stored in the cookie enables that site to compile information about your browsing habits and purchases to help them serve you better. They can also pass this information on to other Web sites. Virtual shopping carts need cookies to complete your online order.

What are some of the most popular search engines?

There are lots of search sites, and more are arriving all the time. Here are a few of the big names.

AltaVista	**www.altavista.com**
Excite	**www.excite.com**
Google	**www.google.com**
HotBot	**www.hotbot.com**
Lycos	**www.lycos.com**
Yahoo!	**www.yahoo.com**

 OW WHERE DO I GO?!

CONTACTS	PUBLICATIONS
Netscape Navigator	**America Online for Dummies**
800-411-0707	By John Kaufeld
(A credit card is required; the charge is $29 per incident, aka problem.)	**Ebay for Dummies**
America Online	By Roland Woerner
888-346-3704	**Internet Auctions for Dummies**
Internet Explorer for Win 9x	By Greg Holden
425-635-7123	

e-mail

E-mail allows you to send and receive letters, messages, or even greeting cards complete with interactive videos.

getting an *e-mail* account

It's just like having your own mailbox in cyberspace

LET'S BE FRANK. THE REAL REASON for signing up with your friendly Internet Service Provider or online service is to get an **e-mail** account. E-mail is computerspeak for electronic mail. This is where you send and receive letters, messages, or even greeting cards complete with interactive videos. There are millions of folks who also have e-mail accounts. There's a good chance some of them are your friends and family.

Once you've gotten your online service set up (see page 168), your provider will offer you an e-mail account. As with everything else in computerland, you need software. **Online software** can be tucked into your **browser software** (the software that lets you use the Internet), or it might be part of your operating system software. For example, if you use the Netscape browser, you might use Netscape Messenger, or you might use Outlook Express, which comes with your Windows operating system.

See that mailbox with a letter sticking out? That's your electronic mailbox. You've got mail. Click on it to read and reply.

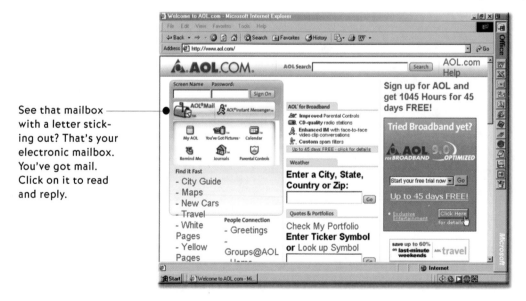

You could also use Eudora Light or Pegasus, both of which are popular e-mail programs for the Internet. (It's a good idea to check with your online provider to see if they have a specific e-mail program they recommend or want you to use and if it costs extra.)

Some providers let you sign up for a free dial-up e-mail account. Yes, FREE! Two popular companies are Juno at **www.juno.com** and NetZero at **www.netzero.net**. To use their e-mail software, you have to download it from the Internet (see page 186). The only drawback to free e-mail is that you will get a lot of electronic advertisements.

ASK THE EXPERTS

How safe is e-mail?

It's not secure from prying eyes. . . e-mail messages are like electronic postcards. Other people can sometimes gain access and read them. And incoming e-mail may not be safe for another reason, because of computer **viruses**. These are manmade computer bugs that are spread via e-mail. If you open an infected e-mail, it can sometimes wreak havoc with your computer. Do not open e-mail messages from people or companies you do not know.

How can companies afford to offer free e-mail?

Advertising is the name of the game. Have you seen those little blinking advertisements that appear on-screen when using your Web browser? Each time you click on one of those blinking advertisements—known as banners—you are being tracked (see pages 179 and 187 for more information on cookies). If you end up buying something from a Web site that the banner "led" you to, that advertiser gets the credit. Banner advertisements are tailored to your specific interests and purchasing habits. When you sign up for free e-mail, be prepared to see a lot of banners.

your e-mail *address*

No more waiting in line at the post office

WHEN YOU SEND E-MAIL, you follow all the similar actions of writing a letter: writing it, addressing it, and placing it in a mailbox—except all these actions are now done on your computer screen in a fraction of the time. Welcome to the new millennium.

Before you can send or receive anything, you need to have an address. Your Internet—rather, your e-mail—address is made up of two parts: your name (some people use their real names; others make up catchy nicknames), and your domain name—technospeak for the name of your e-mail provider, for example, AOL or the Microsoft Network. Note this: These two parts are separated by an @, or "at," sign. For example, here's a typical e-mail address: MaryPrankster@aol.com. Let's decipher it: MaryPrankster is the person's log-on name, and her e-mail account is at the America Online Company, or to use its domain name, aol.com. (Remember ".com" is Internet shorthand for company.) Or in the following address, julie@pets.org, for example, the first part, julie, is the log-on name (like a home address) and pets.org is the domain name. (.org is computer shorthand for a nonprofit organization.)

To send e-mail, you must know the exact Internet address, just as you must know the right address to put on an envelope going through the U.S. mail. The Internet is composed of computers that are linked all over the globe, and each one acts as a post office to route your message to the right destination.

ASK THE EXPERTS

What happens if I get part of an e-mail address wrong?

If you get any part of an e-mail address wrong and send it, it will be returned to you with an error message saying your intended recipient couldn't be found (so you will know to recheck the e-mail address).

Why do some people use lowercase letters in their e-mail addresses?

E-mail addresses are not case sensitive. The computer will read a capital letter or a lowercase letter the same way, so don't worry about whether you should capitalize a name.

Must I use only letters and numbers in my e-mail address, or can I use other characters?

The only other allowable characters in an e-mail address are periods, underscores, and hyphens. For example, mary.prankster; mary_prankster; or mary-prankster. You can't use ampersands (&), slashes (/), or asterisks (*).

LOST AND FOUND

If you want to find the e-mail address of a friend you have lost touch with, you can use the popular Internet Address Finder, which contains around six million addresses. You can access this information online at **www.iaf.net** (that's .net, not .com) by first adding your e-mail address to the list of names. This will help other people find you as well. There are many address locators. Here are two others you can check: **whowhere.lycos.com,** and **people.yahoo.com** (no www. needed).

getting e-mail
messages

*Finally,
you've got
mail!*

OKAY. YOU'VE SIGNED UP and gotten an e-mail account.
Chances are your very first message will be from your online account to
check that all is well. New messages are received in the Inbox of your e-
mail program (think of it as your new inbox on your desk). New, unread
messages are usually displayed in bold type. Messages you have already
read are usually in regular type.

In some programs, when you click on a new-message line, you will be
able to view the message on your computer screen, usually in some sort
of box format. In other programs, you need to double-click on the message to open it into its own window. When you have finished reading
your messages, you can usually close, delete, or send them to someone
else (see page 196). Otherwise they will automatically be stored in your
inbox mail file.

Here's a typical
e-mail box. It tells
you who the e-mail
is from, the subject,
and the date and
time it was received.
Notice how some
e-mails have a paper
clip next to them.
That means an elec-
tronic file (or docu-
ment) is attached
along with it. (See
next page.)

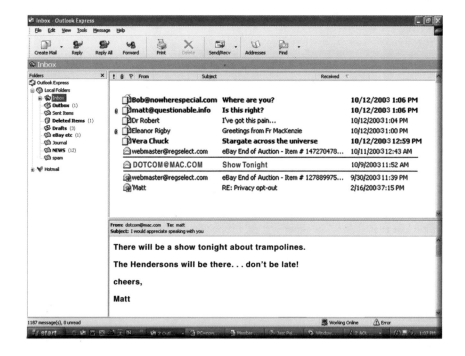

194

ASK THE EXPERTS

How do I reply directly to a message?

Once you open and read a message, you will probably want to reply to it. You can reply to the person who sent you the message (known as the **sender**) by clicking on Reply or Reply to All (if there was more than one recipient).

How do I open an e-mail attachment?

If you see a paper clip or some other symbol next to an e-mail in your inbox, that means it has an attachment to it. When you open your message, you should see an icon, a stamp-sized box with text describing the attached file. To open the attachment, double-click on it. If it doesn't open, you probably don't have the right software to read the file. E-mail a message back to the sender asking how to open it and what software program the file is written in. If there is a .zip after the file name, that means it's been compressed so it can be downloaded, or copied from the Internet, more quickly. To expand it back to normal, you need software called WinZip, which is available at most computer stores.

FIRST PERSON   **DISASTER STORY**

E-Mailer Beware

I love my computer. It's made time-consuming tasks like writing letters to friends and family easy. I used to write these long letters, now I just e-mail away and—bing—off it goes. It's amazing. (I wonder if this is how my grandmother felt when she took her first ride in a Ford Model T.) The only bad thing is that I get a lot of unsolicited e-mail—mostly from people wanting to sell me stuff. But there was one e-mail I'll never forget. It said it was from a discount travel agency. If I opened up the link (the underlined part) in the e-mail message, it would link me to a super discount site for Hawaii. Of course, I did just that. Instead of Hawaii, it kept repeating the message over and over again and I couldn't stop it. Even when I turned off my computer and restarted it, the message was still there. I was so unnerved I called my service provider, who told me that the link to the discount site had a virus which had attacked my computer. They suggested I buy antivirus software and install it and it would kill the virus. I did and was back up and running. The moral: don't open any links from any e-mailer you don't know. It's just like my grandmother used to tell us kids, don't get in a car with a stranger.

—Molly G., Darien, Connecticut

sending
e-mail

All you need to know about communicating via e-mail

WHEN YOU CLICK ON THE COMPOSE OR REPLY BUTTON, it will automatically set up a page to write an e-mail. It will justify the margins and pick the font size, much like a word processor. You can view and compose your e-mail messages by using the following features:

A Print command icon: Use it to print a copy of an e-mail before or after you send it, or print a copy of a received e-mail.

B Send To box: Type the name or address of your e-mail recipient here.

C Copy To box: Use it to forward copies of an e-mail you are about to send.

D Subject box: Use it to give your e-mail a name or title (a must with most e-mail software).

E E-mail tool bar: Use it to change your e-mail style defaults.

F E-mail letter window: Type your e-mail message here.

G Attachments button: Click on it if you want to include an attachment with your message. An Attachment dialogue box will open. Click on Attach, which brings up another dialogue box with all your files listed. Find the file you want to attach and double-click on it. It will be added to your attachment box. Click OK. You will see a disk icon of the file in your e-mail message.

Send Now

Send Now icon: When your e-mail is ready to send, click on it.

Send Later

Send Later icon: Click on it when you want to delay sending your e-mail.

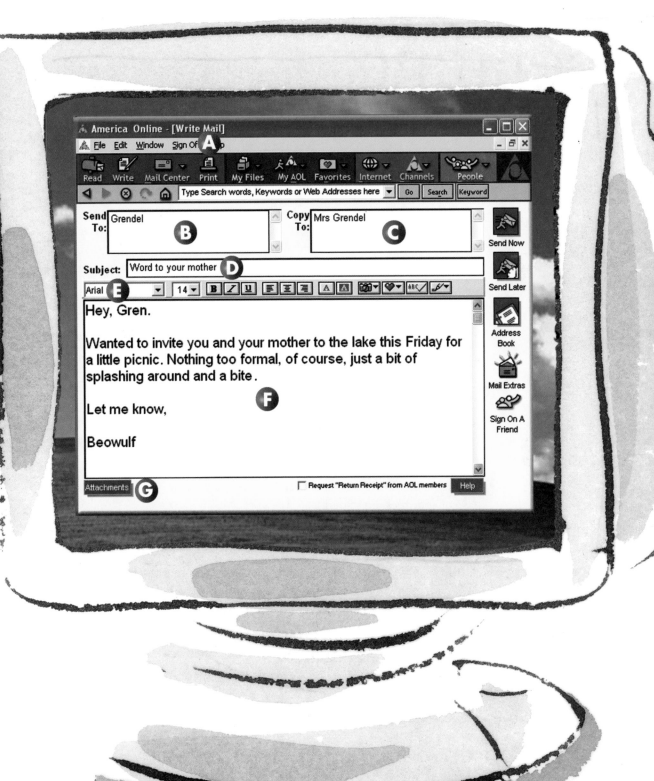

America Online - [Write Mail]

File Edit Window Sign Of___ ___

Read Write Mail Center Print My Files My AOL Favorites Internet Channels People

Type Search words, Keywords or Web Addresses here   Go   Search   Keyword

Send To: Grendel **B**

Copy To: Mrs Grendel **C**

Send Now

Subject: Word to your mother **D**

Arial **E**   14   **B** *I* U   ☰ ☰ ☰   A A

Send Later

Hey, Gren.

Wanted to invite you and your mother to the lake this Friday for a little picnic. Nothing too formal, of course, just a bit of splashing around and a bite.

Address Book

F

Let me know,

Mail Extras

Beowulf

Sign On A Friend

Attachments **G**

☐ Request "Return Receipt" from AOL members   Help

A

sending
attachments

Share your pictures the e-mail way

YOUR COMPUTER'S HARD DRIVE is probably a treasure chest of cool things—ranging from digital pictures of your pets to that first draft of the Great American Novel you've been working on. If you want to share any of the stuff you have there, then e-mail is a great way to do it.

And it's easy to do, too. When you're composing an e-mail message, check out the tool bar at the top of your software for a paper clip icon, or look for some other button labeled Attach or Attachment. Almost all e-mail software has one—even Web-based e-mail services such as HotMail and YahooMail.

SENDING ATTACHMENTS

1. When you click on the Attach button, a dialogue box appears.

2. Check out the drives on your hard disk, and click on the one that contains the file. (The drive labeled C: will be your hard disk, where most of your files are stored.)

3. Look for the folder in which your file is stored, and open it by double-clicking on it.

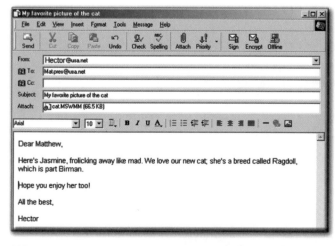

4. When you find the file you want to share, double-click on its icon. Click on OK if the dialogue box is still open.

5. You'll then be returned to the message you were writing, but you'll see a new element on the screen—the name of the file you just attached (and how much memory it takes up).

6. If the wrong file is listed, you probably misclicked in step 4. No problem—just right-click on the attachment, select Delete from the drop-down menu that appears, and start again. That's all. When you send the e-mail, the attachment will go with it.

ASK THE EXPERTS

Why does it take so long to send an e-mail attachment?

The bigger the attachment, the longer it takes to to send. And anything larger than two megabytes (about the size of two 8x10-inch digital photographs) won't go through at all. The smaller the attachment, the faster it goes to the sender.

I have to send a big file! What can I do?

Your only choice is to **compress** the file you have. If you have Windows 95, 98, or 2000, you will need to download a software program called WinZip. This program will both compress files for easy mailing and decompress them back to normal size for viewing. You can also buy it at your computer or office-supply store.

To compress a file, you need first to select the file, then right-click on it (use the *right* button on the mouse). A menu bar will come down. Choose Add to Zip, then follow the WinZip directions. To open a compressed file, you simply click on it and drag it to your desktop, then double-click to open it. (It will uncompress on the way to your desktop.)

If you have Windows Millennium Edition (Windows ME to its friends), you have something like WinZip built in. To use it while you are in your e-mail program, click on the attachment paper clip and find the file you want to attach. Then use the *right* mouse button to click on it and select Send To. Click on the option Compressed Folder, and Windows will shrink the file down into what looks like a folder, but which is actually a file with the same name but with the extension .zip. Now click the Attach button.

now what do I do?

Answers to common questions

Someone wrote "BFN" in an e-mail to me. What does this mean?

"BFN" means Bye For Now. There are many common acronyms used in e-mail because they take up so much less space than writing out the phrase. Here are some others:

ATB	All the best	LOL	Laughing out loud
BTW	By the way	OTF	On the floor (laughing)
FWIW	For what it's worth	TIA	Thanks in advance
FYI	For your information	TTFN	Ta Ta for now
IMHO	In my humble opinion	TTYL	Talk to you later
IMO	In my opinion		

How do I e-mail the same group of people?

Groups are lists of e-mail addresses that you can create when there is a particular set of people you regularly want e-mail messages to go to. For example, if you like sending jokes to all your friends, you might want to create a Jokes group that contains all the e-mail addresses of your friends. In your address book, simply click the New Group option and select the names or type the addresses of the people you want in the group. Then, when you want to send a message to all those people, you only have to click on the group name, not each individual e-mail address.

What do some of the smiley faces mean in e-mail messages?

The following are a few known emoticons, which are "emotions" + "icons":

:-)	A smile	;-)	A wink
8-)	Goofy smile—or glasses	:-&	Tongue-tied
:-(	Sadness, disapproval	:-p	Tongue stuck out

How can I have my computer tell me when I get an e-mail?

When you are online, depending on your e-mail program, new messages might pop up automatically. If not, you will have to click the Send/Receive button on the button bar.

What happens to e-mail messages when I delete them?

Each e-mail program treats read e-mails differently. Click once to highlight the e-mail message line in your Inbox and press the Delete key on the keyboard. Depending on your e-mail program, your message will either be gone for good or remain temporarily in a Deleted Items folder (similar to the Windows Recycle Bin) waiting for you to right-click and empty the bin for good.

How can I forward a message to someone else?

Sometimes after you read an e-mail message, you may want to forward it to another person. For example, you receive a funny joke from your aunt and want your best friend to read it as well. In that case, you can forward the message to that person. When you click the Forward button, the message will usually remain at the bottom of the e-mail—unless you have instructed your e-mail not to do that in the preferences area. Then, fill out the new-message box just as you would a new message. Try to add a sentence or two that explains why you're forwarding the message.

 **N**OW WHERE DO I GO?!

CONTACTS	PUBLICATIONS
Microsoft Outlook Express	**E-mail for Dummies**
425-635-7056	By John B. Levine
Netscape Mail	
800-411-0707	
(A credit card is required; the charge	
is $29 per incident, aka problem.)	
America Online	
888-346-3704	

estate planning

" *I drafted a will about 15 years ago, so I'm all set, right?* "

your *estate*

Divvying up your stuff

MAYBE YOU THINK THAT ESTATE PLANNING IS for rich retired people. Perhaps you have a plan in place, but you haven't reviewed it lately. Now that you've retired, it's important to start thinking about how you want your property to be divided up after you're gone. You finally have time to review all your legal issues and create what estate planners call an "exit strategy." Your planning is sure to save your heirs money, time, and heartache.

The box below spells out different ways that your possessions pass to your heirs. An estate-planning attorney can be invaluable in helping you get the paperwork done.

<table>
<tr><td colspan="2">RED FLAG

The biggest mistake people (even rich ones) make in estate planning is not realizing that joint tenancy and beneficiary designations on insurance and IRAs override any provisions in a will or a trust.</td><td>How asset is held</td><td>Examples</td><td>How it Works</td></tr>
</table>

How asset is held	Examples	How it Works
Joint tenancy or Tenancy by the Entirety (common for married people who own real estate)	Houses, cars, checking accounts, investments, etc.	Assets pass directly to the other joint tenant at your death, regardless of what wills or trusts say.
Beneficiary Designations	Life insurance, 401(k) plans, IRAs	Assets pass directly to the named beneficiary at your death, regardless of what wills or trusts say.
Payable on Death (POD) Designations	Bank accounts, investment accounts	Assets pass directly to the named beneficiary at your death, regardless of what wills or trusts say.
Wills	Assets not held in joint tenancy and without a beneficiary, such as artwork, jewelry, computers	Assets pass to those named in your will, after proceeding through the court system in a process called "probate" (see page 206).
Trusts	Same type of assets as those covered in wills, joint tenancy, or POD	Assets pass to those named in your trust. No court probate process is required.
Intestate (not held in joint tenancy, no beneficiary or POD, no will or trust)	Same type of assets as those covered in wills, joint tenancy, or POD	Assets pass to heirs in the order designated by state laws. Requires court proceedings to determine proper heirs.

YOUR ESTATE

Use this chart to help you identify your assets and liabilities. Start by listing their approximate value. Date the list and put it in a fireproof box in your home. Tell your heirs where you keep it.

ASSETS	ACCOUNT NAME AND NUMBER	APPROX. VALUE
Financial Assets		
Bank accounts	_____	_____
Stocks	_____	_____
Bonds	_____	_____
Mutual Funds	_____	_____
401(k)s	_____	_____
Individual Retirement Accounts (IRAs)	_____	_____
Annuities	_____	_____
Home	_____	_____
Other Real Estate	_____	_____
Life Insurance Death Benefit	_____	_____
Other Financial Assets	_____	_____
Other Assets		
Cars	_____	_____
Jewelry, Watches	_____	_____
Computer Equipment	_____	_____
Furniture	_____	_____
Antiques, Art, Collectibles	_____	_____
Other Assets	_____	_____
TOTAL ASSETS:		
Less: Liabilities		
Mortgage	_____	_____
Credit Card Debt	_____	_____
Taxes	_____	_____
Auto Loans	_____	_____
Student Loans	_____	_____
Other Loans	_____	_____
TOTAL LIABILITIES:	_____	_____
NET ESTATE VALUE:	_____	_____
(TOTAL ASSETS MINUS TOTAL LIABILITIES)	_____	_____

wills

They help ensure that your wishes will be respected

AFTER YOU FIGURE OUT WHAT YOUR ASSETS ARE and where you want them to go, how do you make sure your bequests will happen? Drafting a **will** is the first step. A will specifies who gets your money and property after you die. It names a person to handle your affairs—known as the **executor**; and if you have any children who are minors or disabled, your will needs to name a **guardian** who will look out for their welfare in your stead.

What if you die without a will? It's known as dying **intestate**. When that happens, the government takes control of your estate and a court decides who gets your assets, based on the laws of the state where you live. This can be a long and very public process, and by the time your heirs see any money, a chunk of it is likely to have gone to the court-appointed lawyers.

You can make a will by yourself; legal kits, books, and software can give you instructions. But it is wise to have an estate-planning attorney review your work to help you avoid pitfalls such as willing property that is jointly owned (a common mistake).

No matter how you decide to spell out your last will and testament, nothing is engraved in stone while you are alive. So if circumstances change during your lifetime, you can modify your will at any time.

WHAT IS PROBATE?

The job of the probate court is to make sure your will has been signed and witnessed correctly, that all your taxes and debts have been paid, and that your documented wishes are carried out. Your executor oversees this public process, usually with an attorney's help. This can take anywhere from a few weeks to a year, depending on your estate's complexity (and the court's efficiency), and will incur court costs, filing fees, and recording fees. A trust (see page 212) allows you to bypass probate.

ASK THE EXPERTS

What's a living will?

It's a document explaining your general wishes about your own health care in case you are incapacitated and unable to make decisions for yourself (see page 210).

My spouse and I will leave our assets to each other, and then to our children. Will there be any estate taxes to pay?

It's important in drawing up your wills to work out how to minimize any tax bite that might diminish what you leave behind. No taxes are due when the first spouse dies, since you can pass unlimited assets to your spouse without any tax consequences. When your assets ultimately pass to your kids, however, they'll incur taxes if your estate exceeds certain levels. Estate taxes can usually be avoided by properly structuring your wills and trusts.

I hear that estate tax laws might be repealed. Shouldn't I wait until this is final before doing any planning?

Even though the laws regarding estate taxation are being repealed, you still need to plan your estate now. Saving estate taxes is just one part of estate planning.

PARTNERSPEAK

It's especially important to discuss your will with your spouse. And don't hesitate to involve a qualified estate-planning attorney to help you do it more efficiently. Once your plan is in place, make sure your spouse understands the details and the location of the will and all the related documents. It is also a good idea to review your intentions about what you want to happen if you die versus if you become incapacitated.

FIRST PERSON · DISASTER STORY

When the Will Doesn't Count

I grew up in a beautiful home that I'd always dreamed of owning. I often talked to Mom and Dad about my desire to live there one day. After Mom died, Dad remarried, but he assured me that he had arranged for the home to eventually be mine. After his death, I was shocked to learn that his new wife was selling it. Turns out that although Dad did specify in his will that the house should go to me, he had retitled the home in joint tenancy with his wife. That meant that the will didn't apply, and the house passed to her.

— **Sara E., Willow Springs, Illinois**

the *executor's* job

YOU'LL NEED TO DECIDE WHO WILL OVERSEE the transfer of your assets to your heirs. If you're married, you'll probably choose your spouse as your **executor**. But what if you're single? Or if you and your spouse die at the same time? Who should handle all of your affairs? If you choose one of your children, nieces, or nephews, who will you choose?

Before you decide on your executor, look at what the job entails. Talk to the person you choose as executor to make sure he or she feels equal to the task. Go over a copy of your will, so that you can answer any questions your executor might have.

The executor:
- Opens and inventories your safe-deposit box.
- Gets copies of your death certificate and distributes them to the insurance companies, banks, and other institutions where your assets are located.
- Files your will with probate court if necessary.
- Inventories all of your assets and insurance policies.
- Sells any assets and household goods that must be disposed of.
- Pays all of your debts and any income taxes owed the year you died.
- Keeps funeral expense records.
- Notifies the Social Security Administration of your death with a copy of the death certificate, and finds out if any survivor benefits are available.
- Hires any necessary professionals to help in the process of settling the estate: lawyers, accountants, or investment professionals.

- Gets the full names, addresses, and Social Security numbers of everyone named in the will or trust and distributes the inheritance according to the document's instructions.
- Puts a death notice in the local newspaper.

 SK THE EXPERTS

I drafted a will about 15 years ago, so I'm all set, right?
Not necessarily. Because of changes in your family status, financial situation, and estate-tax laws, your estate-planning documents should be reviewed every few years. Also, if you move out of state, your documents need to change to reflect the laws where you live.

What if I need to change my will after it's been drafted?
Changes to wills are called **codicils**. They are necessary for any major changes, such as the birth of another child or the sale of an important asset listed in the will. Codicils need to be written out, signed by you and two witnesses, and added to the will.

Can I avoid the probate process?
Yes. If you have an "I Love You" will giving all of your assets to your spouse, your estate probably won't need to go through probate or be required to pay any estate taxes (see page 207). Also, any assets that are in joint tenancy, or have a named beneficiary, or are "payable on death" will avoid probate since these assets pass directly to the heir without being subject to your will or probate. But the remaining spouse will not have the luxury of avoiding probate, so it might be a good idea for both husband and wife to set up living trusts (see pages 212–213), not only to avoid probate but to keep the estate from being diminished by estate taxes when the second spouse dies.

CHECKLIST FOR CHOOSING AN EXECUTOR
- You trust the person.
- The person is geographically close to your assets and records.
- The person has time to devote to your estate.
- The person is capable of handling all the necessary tasks.

PAYING THE EXECUTOR

The executor is generally allowed to take a small percentage of your estate (about 2 percent) as payment for the services that must be rendered. Close family members often do not take such a payment, however, unless the work is exceptionally demanding, because they are often beneficiaries of the will.

You may choose your lawyer or your bank to act as your executor, in which case a percentage is usually determined ahead of time. If you do not choose any executor, an administrator will be chosen by the probate court to act as an executor, and will be paid a percentage of your estate as determined by the court.

power of *attorney*

If your affairs need looking after while you're alive

BY NOW YOU'VE PONDERED HOW THINGS might be handled when you go. But what happens if tragedy strikes and leaves you mentally or physically incapacitated? Who will make decisions on your behalf? More important, who will be recognized by the government, doctors, and the business world as empowered to make decisions for you?

By having a few simple documents on hand, you can solve this dilemma. The person you give **power of attorney** (POA) to will legally be able to look after your interests, should you become unable to do it for yourself. There are two basic types of power of attorney, one to cover your finances, another to cover your health. The documents vary from state to state, so be sure to discuss the details with an attorney. Here are the basics:

PROPERTY POWER OF ATTORNEY This document allows you to name someone, called your **agent**, to make financial decisions for you if you are unable to make them for yourself. This can either be effective immediately, or you can have it take effect once your doctor certifies that you're unable to give prompt and intelligent attention to your affairs. For example, if you were in a coma and your spouse needed to sell your jointly held home, having a property power of attorney in place (with your spouse named as your agent) would allow him or her to sign on your behalf.

HEALTHCARE POWER OF ATTORNEY This document allows you to name someone, called your agent or representative, to make decisions on your behalf regarding your medical treatment. It also grants powers regarding autopsy and organ donation in the event of your death, and it allows you to document your feelings about life support and under what circumstances to pursue it.

 SK THE EXPERTS

What's the difference between a living will and a healthcare power of attorney? Do I need both?

A living will communicates the specific medical treatment you want (most often regarding the level of life support) should you become unable to discuss this with your doctor yourself. The power of attorney document names a person to make decisions on your behalf about any aspects of your health care not specified in the living will. Here's the catch: Even though living wills can be more difficult to make operative, they have precedence over the power of attorney. This is why some lawyers suggest having only a POA. That way your representative can make decisions in response to all situations that might arise, including your wishes about specific treatments such as extended life support.

What's an involuntary conservatorship?

If you have not signed a power of attorney document, a greedy relative or even a nursing home might convince a judge that you cannot care for yourself. If the judge awards an involuntary conservatorship to such an agent, you could lose the rights to your income, your assets, your car—and even your right to vote. But by having a power of attorney document, you can insure that someone you trust will be the only conservator of your affairs.

I am widowed. Who should I choose to act as my healthcare POA? A close relative? My executor?

It is a question of who might be attentive if you are sick, and whose judgment you can rely on. If you were to be sent to the hospital with a serious ailment, who would visit you most often there? Is that person someone you can trust to make major healthcare decisions for you? Your executor might be a good choice, provided he or she would be available if you are ill. If you happen to have a close friend who is a doctor or nurse, that person might also be a possible choice.

trusts

Legal arrangements to keep your assets out of probate court

A TRUST IS ANOTHER WAY OF OWNING your property and distributing it to your heirs. An especially nifty feature of trusts is that they allow your estate's assets to pass directly to your heirs—without subjecting them to the time and expense of the probate process (see page 206).

LIVING TRUSTS are the most common type of trust—they can act as a will substitute. A living trust costs more for your attorney to create than a will, but if it keeps your estate from being dragged through the probate court, it could be money well spent.

If you have a significant estate (more than $2,000,000), some trusts, like credit shelter trusts (see page 215), irrevocable life insurance trusts, and charitable trusts, can actually save you estate taxes.

There are generally three parties to a trust:

The grantor: The person who gives the assets to the trust.
The trustee: The person who makes sure that the trust's instructions are followed.
The beneficiaries: Those who receive the assets from the trust.

If you create a living trust, you are the grantor, the trustee, *and* the beneficiary while you're still alive. At your death, the trustee you named as successor will take over implementing the trust, and the trust's assets will pass to your beneficiaries according to your wishes.

	WILLS	LIVING TRUSTS
WHO ARE THE PARTIES INVOLVED?	**Testator**—You, the person who makes the will. **Executor**—A person who administers the will after your death.	**Grantor**—You, the person who transfers property. **Trustee**—A person who legally owns the property once the grantor has transferred property title to the trust. (With a living trust, this can also be you.) **Beneficiary**—A person who inherits the assets from the trust.
WHEN DOES THE DOCUMENT TAKE EFFECT?	Once you sign the will before witnesses, it is legal, but it doesn't take effect until you die.	Once a living trust is signed, and you transfer assets to the trust, it is in effect.
WHAT HAPPENS WHEN YOU DIE?	The will becomes irrevocable, and the executor carries out its provisions. The will must go through the probate process, which the public has access to, and which can be costly and time-consuming. (Probate may be bypassed if all of the assets pass to the spouse.)	The revocable trust becomes irrevocable, and the trustee you designated carries out its provisions privately, without court supervision.
WHAT IF YOU BECOME INCAPACITATED DURING YOUR LIFETIME?	Since it doesn't become effective until after your death, the will can't be used to indicate your preferences should you become incapacitated.	A living trust can designate how your affairs should be handled in the event of incapacity.

tax
consequences
for your heirs

Plan ahead, and the government won't take as much

ON TOP OF ALL THE PROFESSIONAL FEES, court costs, and other expenses you might get hit with, your beneficiaries might have to pay estate taxes. As of 2003, if the total value of your estate (financial assets as well as the appraised value of your home, cars, art, jewelry, etc.) is less than $1 million, relax: estate taxes probably won't apply to you. If it's more than $1 million—and you're concerned about minimizing the estate's tax liability—keep reading. (In 2004, the number rises to $1.5 million.)

With estate tax rates starting at 37 percent and quickly climbing to nearly 50 percent, these taxes can take a huge bite out of assets you leave to your loved ones—but only the amount exceeding the $1 million cutoff.

Here's what you need to know:

● Any and all assets you leave to a spouse or a charity are not subject to estate taxes.

● Once you deduct assets left to a spouse or a charity, only the portion of your remaining assets that exceed the $1 million limit are subject to estate tax.

● If you're married and both your estates are structured properly, you can potentially leave a combined $2 million ($3 million in 2004 and 2005) to your children without paying estate taxes.

● Say you leave 100 percent of your property to a spouse. Sure, no estate taxes are taken out, but you've lost a chance to leave $1 million worth of tax-free assets to heirs other than your spouse. The result? When your spouse dies, only the portion of your joint estate covered by your spouse's exclusion of $1 million will pass tax free to heirs. If you, too, had left up to $1 million's worth to heirs other than your spouse, you could have used the full $2 million exclusion allowed for a married couple.

OPTIONS FOR MINIMIZING TAXES

If your estate is large enough for estate taxes to be a concern, talk to an estate-planning attorney about whether any of these techniques might benefit your heirs. See chapter 13 for more details.

Gifts: If you're leaving money to family and friends, consider giving them part of their inheritance while you're still alive. (They don't pay income tax on these gifts, but you do if it's over a certain amount.) Giving money away helps to deplete your estate, not to mention provides you with the chance to see your loved ones enjoy the money. Uncle Sam lets you give away up to $11,000 per person per year, without any tax consequences (estate or personal) to you or to them. If you give more than that, you'll need to file a gift tax return (see box).

Charitable Donations: Consider leaving at least a portion of your estate to your favorite charity. Assets left to a charity escape any and all taxes. In fact, if you set up a trust for a charity during your lifetime, you'll get an income tax deduction at that time. Better still, you can receive income from the trust as long as you live. At your death the money would pass—estate-tax free—to the charity.

Credit Shelter Trust: If the estate you and your spouse will leave behind is at least $2 million, you might want to set up a **Credit Shelter Trust** (also known as a Bypass Trust or an A-B Trust). This allows $1 million of a couple's estate to go into a trust for the children (or other heirs) when the first spouse dies. All assets exceeding the $1 million flow to the surviving spouse, who can also use any income generated by the trust. When the surviving spouse dies, the second $1 million exclusion is applied to the remaining estate. But before setting up this trust, you must be sure that your spouse won't need the first $1 million principal that will be shielded in the trust.

GIVING MORE THAN $11,000

You can give your assets away in any amounts you wish, whenever you wish. However, if you give more than $11,000 in any year to a single recipient, be sure to file IRS form 709. This tax return tracks your gifts and calculates the tax you owe if you give away more than allowed each year.

funeral planning

Work out the details in advance

IT'S UNCOMFORTABLE TO THINK ABOUT your own death and the arrangements your family would have to make for you. But, because such choices are rarely discussed beforehand, your survivors are left to make costly decisions when they are least able to think straight. Fortunately, prearranged funerals seem to be on the upswing. With a little advance planning on your part, family and friends will be relieved of the important decisions and will feel secure that they're doing what you would have wanted.

There are two ways you can help prearrange your funeral:

- Preplan. By doing your funeral and burial homework in advance, you can lay out your preferences ahead of time. Here are the main choices to consider: Do you want to be buried or cremated? Do you want a simple or top-of-the-line casket? Which cemetery do you prefer? Documenting the products and services that you want and discussing them with your family ahead of time will help them during a very stressful time. Some folks even set up a bank account earmarked for these future expenses.

- Prepay. This takes preplanning a step further by contracting with a funeral home, cemetery, and/or casket dealer, and providing payment in advance. In order for people to feel comfortable with this arrangement, most contracts can be funded with a trust, annuity, or burial insurance policy to ensure that the money will be available when needed. If you go this route, make sure you understand how the arrangement is funded, and then let your loved ones know. Also, carefully review any cancellation policies, in case you change your mind later on.

Give instructions to your family so they can access the policy, receipts, and plans you have made when needed. By the way, your safe-deposit box is not a good place to keep such information because it might be sealed for weeks in the event of your death (unless the box is held jointly). A fireproof box or file at home would be more convenient.

ASK THE EXPERTS

What does a funeral entail and how much does it cost?

A funeral home provides a variety of goods and services, including planning assistance, care of the body, transporting it to and from the funeral home, and use of the funeral home and equipment for wakes, visitation, and even the funeral itself. The industry average for these goods and services (including a casket) is about $5,000. Note: Caskets can be the most expensive part of a funeral. Caskets are made from a wide variety of wood or metals and lined with either velvet or crepe. Prices range from $600 or so for a simple pine box to elaborate caskets exceeding $7,000. Additional items to consider include fees for the clergy, organist, and other musicians, obituary fees, cost of flowers and thank-you notes, and limo transportation for the family. These can add up to $1,000 to the cost of a funeral.

I heard that burial vaults are more expensive than grave liners. What's the difference?

Grave liners are required by most cemeteries to keep the ground from settling over time. Burial vaults serve the same purpose, but are made of concrete or other solid materials so they also protect the casket. These can range anywhere from $500 to $2,000 or more.

How can I get costs up front from the local funeral homes?

The FTC requires funeral homes to provide general price lists (by telephone or in person) for each product and service they provide. Call several local funeral homes and get their price lists so you can compare costs.

now what do I do?

Answers to common questions

How do I choose an attorney to help me plan my estate?

Start by getting names of estate-planning attorneys from friends and family. Interview likely candidates, asking about the process that would be used to prepare your estate and the fees involved. Find out about the attorney's background, education, experience, and areas of specialization. Does he or she work with many clients whose demographics are similar to yours? And whose estate size is similar to yours? Finally, assess how you feel when talking with this attorney. Do you feel comfortable or talked down to?

I have shares of Sears stock my granddad bought for me when I was born. They're now worth over $100,000. What are the most efficient ways to leave the stock to a charity or to my heirs?

Whatever you do, don't sell the shares to give the proceeds away. That would subject you to capital gains tax on the difference between the purchase price and the sale price. For estate-planning purposes, here are two alternatives. First, consider giving the shares themselves to a charity. By donating the shares, 1) you get an income tax deduction for the shares' current value; 2) you don't pay capital gains tax on the gain; and 3) the charity can sell the shares without tax consequences. Or, if you will the stock to your heirs when you die, they could sell it immediately and pay no capital gains tax. Heirs are "assumed" to have bought the stock on the day you died for its current price. The "assumed" price equals the sales price, so no tax would be due. But if you give it to your heirs before you die, and they sell it immediately, they would pay capital gains tax because the "assumed" price is what the price was when you bought it.

This is my second marriage, so I'm concerned about providing for my children from my first marriage.

Your attorney might recommend a Qualified Terminable Interest Property trust (also known as a Q-TIP). This trust allows you to pass property to your spouse when you die—but requires the property to pass to your children after your spouse dies.

What should I look for in a funeral parlor?

First of all, consider a funeral parlor whose location is convenient to the family members. You should also consider the home's reputation for service, and any personal experience you've had at other people's funerals. Given the high cost of funerals, the fees must be considered, too.

 **N**OW WHERE DO I GO?!

CONTACTS

www.nolo.com/lawcenter/ency
Look for user-friendly articles on a variety of estate planning topics.

www.smartmoney.com/estate

**National Network
of Estate Planning Attorneys**
One Valmont Plaza
Fourth Floor
Omaha, NB 68154
Tel: 888-337-4090
Fax: 888-872-8721
www.netplanning.com/consumer

American Academy of Estate Planning
9360 Towne Centre Drive
Suite 300
San Diego, CA 92121
Tel: 800-846-1555
www.aaepa.com

**National Association of Financial &
Estate Planning**
525 E. 4500 South, F-100
Salt Lake City, UT 84107
Tel: 801-266-9900
Fax: 801-266-1019
www.nafep.com

**International Cemetery and
Funeral Association**
1895 Preston White Drive
Reston, VA 20191
800-645-7700
www.icfa.org

PUBLICATIONS

Wealth: Enhancement & Preservation
by Robert A. Esperti and Renno L. Peterson

**Caring for the Dead: Your Final Act
of Love**
by Lisa Carlson

gift *planning*

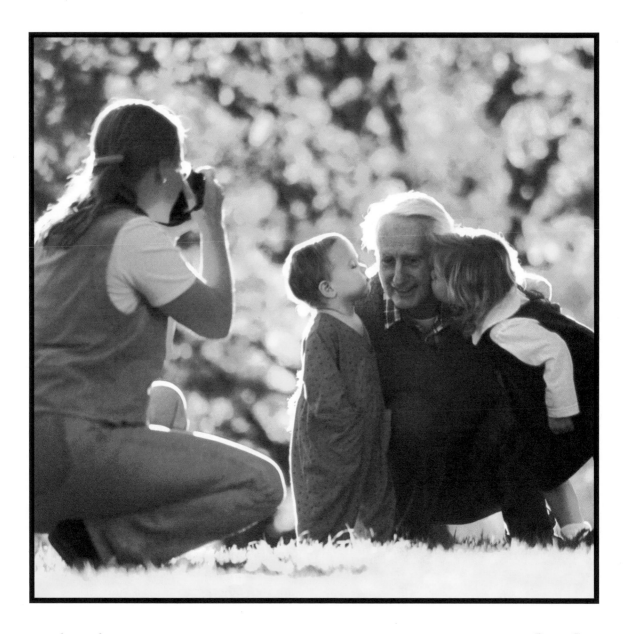

The IRS offers unlimited gift tax exclusions when you pay someone else's medical or education bills.

giving *gifts*

Help your heirs now,
and save on taxes later

BY DRAWING UP A LEGALLY BINDING WILL, you stipulate who gets your money and all your other earthly possessions. (See page 206.) But what if you want to see your beneficiaries enjoying their inheritance (and your generosity) while you're still alive? No matter what your age or income level, you can **gift**, or give away, just about anything: cash, stocks, and bonds, your life insurance policy, even your IRA. (Of course, before doing so, you should discuss this with an estate planner, an attorney, or

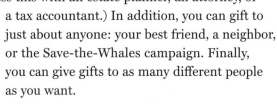

a tax accountant.) In addition, you can gift to just about anyone: your best friend, a neighbor, or the Save-the-Whales campaign. Finally, you can give gifts to as many different people as you want.

Gifting during your lifetime can save you and your heirs big bucks on taxes, too. How so? The government levies a substantial tax on money and property (above a certain amount) that you leave to your heirs when you die. By sharing your wealth with others you decrease the total value of your estate (thereby reducing the estate taxes owed on it). Better still, the gifts you make during your lifetime are tax free to your heirs. No wonder gifting is such a popular estate-planning strategy.

Ask THE EXPERTS

One of my four sons needs money to make a down payment on a house and to cover some mortgage payments. Should I gift it to him outright and then deduct it from his inheritance?

It's up to you. Gifting money to your children can be simply that—a gift. The good thing about gifting money is that it lowers the value of your estate, which thereby lowers the amount of any estate tax your heirs may owe. So in that sense, money you give to one child now may benefit all your heirs. However, to keep things fair betwen your sons, you may prefer to deduct the amount you give your one son now from his inheritance. Obviously, if you do this, you'll want to keep good records of the amounts given, the dates, etc. To avoid any confusion, you will also have to decide the best way to give this money to your son. Your attorney can help you sort through the details.

My daughter is behind on her new car payments. I'd like to help her, but would that help or send the wrong message?

It's always good to consider the emotional ramifications of financial decisions that affect family members. First, consider who started the dialogue. Did she approach you about it or was it your idea? If she is the one asking, consider whether giving her money now will allow her to get her finances in order or just give her an easy out. If helping her out was your idea, ask yourself if you might be meddling a bit too much. The best way to handle this is to sit down and discuss the matter honestly with your daughter. You might want to consider a partial payment that will help cover some of her debt, but still keep her responsible for the rest. If you do decide to give her money, be sure to file a gift tax return (form 709) with the IRS so you can lower the value of your estate.

QUICK LINKS

For more on estate planning, go to:

www.estateplanninglinks.com
Calculators, forms, and links to helpful sites

www.quicken.com
130 articles on estate planning; search for estate planning on the home page.

how much can you *give?*

The magic $11,000 number

THE GOVERMENT ENCOURAGES YOU TO BE GENEROUS TO FAMILY AND FRIENDS. The federal tax code allows you to give up to $11,000 to anyone, once a year, without incurring any gift tax. If you're married, you and your spouse can each give $11,000— that's $22,000 from the two of you—per year. And while the total tax-free amount you can give to one person is capped, the number of gifts you can give is not. You could give annual gifts to 100 different people, for example, as long as no one receives more than that magic amount.

When it comes to your husband or wife, the tax code is even more generous with the amount you can give. During your lifetime (or upon your

death), you can give an unlimited amount of money and property to your spouse without incurring any federal estate or gift taxes. This is called the **unlimited marital deduction**. No matter how much money you give to your spouse, it won't be taxed by Uncle Sam.

There is also an unlimited gift tax exclusion when you pay someone else's medical or education bills. The recipient of your largess does not have to be a member of your immediate family or even a relative. However, you must pay the expenses directly to the hospital, doctor, or university. While this process may feel more like bill paying than good old-fashioned gift giving, keep in mind that even though your checks are being mailed to a third party, ultimately you're still making a tax-free gift to your beneficiary.

GIFTING CASE STUDY: THE SCHAEFERS OF CROSS CREEK, FLORIDA

Richard Schaefer, 86, and Helen Schaefer, 83, have three grown children, five grandchildren, and two great-grandchildren. They have been working with an estate planner to decide the best way to distribute their assets, both now and after their deaths.

The couple has invested wisely over the years. Besides their retirement home in Florida, they own the family home in Michigan as well as a small apartment building. Decades ago, they started investing in various stocks and bonds. As a result, their net estate is now valued at $1.7 million.

Upon their deaths, the Schaefers' heirs would receive the money and property as set out in their estate plan, minus the hefty federal tax on bequests (though certain items like funeral expenses and debt payments are excluded). However, this tax applies only to bequests from estates that are, in 2004, worth $1.5 million or more. As the Schaefers' estate is worth $1.7 million, the portion of their estate that exceeds the $1.5 million exemption, or $200,000, would be subject to estate tax.

Based on their lawyer's advice, they've decided to reduce the size of their estate by taking advantage of the annual gift-tax exclusion. They will give each of their 10 descendants $22,000, putting the money in trust for the younger ones. In a single year, they will have given away $220,000 ($22,000 multiplied by 10) gift-tax free. As an added bonus, none of the recipients will have to pay gift tax either. So, in a single year, they will have lowered the amount of their (potentially taxable) estate to $1.48 million—and the money will already be in the hands of their heirs. As the years go on, they will continue making gifts to new arrivals to the family or to existing members to insure that the total value of their estate stays below $1.5 million.

giving
appreciated
property

Should you give away the ranch, too?

WHEN PEOPLE TALK ABOUT GIFTING, they generally mean cash. But you can gift property, too, as well as stocks and bonds. Like cash gifts, gifts of property will reduce the value of your estate. And from an estate-tax planning perspective, that may be a smart move. Why? Because property that you expect to appreciate substantially in value over time can increase the size of your estate dramatically, which means your estate will be subject to even steeper taxes. If you give that property now, however, you will not only remove the asset, but also the asset's future growth, from your estate.

Gifts of stocks and bonds can be a wise idea too. Ordinarily, when you sell stocks and bonds, you pay a **capital gains tax**. That tax is based on the difference between the price you paid for the stock or bond and its appreciated value. If you buy a stock for $100 and sell it for $400, you owe a capital gains tax on the $300 increase in value. (Conversely, if you lose money on your investment—say the stock is now worth $50 when you sell it—you can claim a capital loss on your tax return.)

Furthermore, gifting any appreciated investment from your estate lowers the amount of your estate, which in turn lowers the inheritance tax your heirs may owe on it. While the IRS is generous about gifting, it's not all that generous. It still wants its capital gains tax. That must be paid by the recipient of your gift whenever he or she decides to sell the gifted stock. What about gifting depreciated property? Neither you nor your beneficiary will get to deduct the depreciation from taxes owed. You can only get that if you sell it yourself and claim the loss on your taxes, but that may be a smart thing to do if it ultimately lowers the overall value of your estate.

TO GIFT OR NOT TO GIFT

If you gift appreciated investments, the recipients will have to pay capital gains tax. But if you leave those investments to your heirs in your will, they will be added to the total value of your estate, and so subject to estate tax. So what's the smarter tax-saving strategy, gifting those investments or leaving them in your estate? It depends on a number of variables, but in many cases it's probably wiser to leave those investments in your estate. Why? Because then your heirs can take advantage of a nifty little IRS perk, called the **step-up in basis rule**, which essentially lets them avoid paying any capital gains tax.

Here is an example: Joan bought some stock for $5,000 10 years ago. When she died on August 2, the stock was worth $12,050. In her will, she left the stock to her son Paul. If Paul sells it on August 3, he will get $12,050 and pay no capital gains tax, thanks to the step-up in basis rule. But say that Paul decides to sell the stock two years later, at which point it is worth $15,000. Paul would then have to pay capital gains tax, but only on the $2,950 increase on the price of the stock from the day he inherited it.

FIRST PERSON · SUCCESS STORY

Gifted Grandchildren

When my wife and I realized that our son was struggling to pay the college tuition for our two grandsons, we wanted to help out. The trouble was, our son is not known for being thrifty, and we didn't want to see our money used on anything but college tuition. I felt awkward about discussing this with him, because it would sound like I didn't trust him. Luckily, our attorney saved the day by suggesting that we gift the money to the boys instead, by writing a check directly to the university. That way, we would be sure the money was being used as we wanted. And because we were giving directly to the school, we were not limited by the regular gift tax rules and could be as generous as our wallets allowed. Best of all, we don't ever have to worry that the money isn't going to be used for its intended purpose.

—**Brian G., Memphis, Tennessee**

giving to *charity*

Feeling especially generous this year? Or just wary of sharing your wealth with spendthrift relations? Consider making a gift to your favorite charity. Not only will you get that warm, fuzzy feeling from supporting a worthwhile cause, but you'll save a lot on taxes, too. And, while a gift of cash is the easiest and most frequent way of giving to charity, you can also donate appreciated stock, your IRA—even your insurance policy.

Do a little good and save on taxes

Charitable gifts can be very, very attractive in a number of ways:

1. The money gifted to a charity is not subject to gift and estate taxes. (It doesn't matter if you give this money upon your death or during your lifetime.)

2. The amount you can give to a charity is unlimited. (Remember that if you give to friends or relatives, you can only give up to $11,000 tax free annually, or $22,000 as a married couple.)

3. Gifts made to your favorite charity often qualify for a deduction on your income tax return.

4. With gifts of appreciated property, such as stocks or real estate, you can avoid paying capital gains tax.

5. You can make a charitable gift and then arrange to receive an income stream from that gift for the rest of your life (see page 229).

What qualifies as a charity? Qualified, or tax-exempt, charitable organizations, as defined by the IRS in IRC Section 501(c)(3), may be organized around religious, educational, scientific, or literary work; they may also be involved with improving public safety, fostering national or international amateur sports competition, and preventing cruelty to animals and children, among other causes.

PLANNED GIVING PROGRAMS

Although they were originally designed as a tax-saving option for wealthy folks, planned giving programs have become more mainstream in recent years. These programs, which include charitable remainder trusts and charitable gift annuities, are offered by many well-known charities. Taxpayers like them because they let you take an up-front charitable deduction, receive investment income, save on estate taxes, and, with appreciated property, avoid paying capital gains tax—all in the name of giving to a worthy cause.

Here's how they work:

Let's say that you have stock worth $50,000, which you bought 25 years ago for $5,000. If you were to sell those shares tomorrow, you would have to pay capital gains tax on $45,000 (the difference between the purchase price and the sale price).

Instead, you decide to give the shares to a charitable remainder trust and name your favorite charity as the beneficiary. When the trust sells your stock, it pays no tax on the investment gains because the charity is a tax-exempt entity. The proceeds are then invested, and from this you and your spouse draw set income for the rest of your lives—or for a specified term. You can then deduct a portion of the full market value of your donation (depending on your age and the amount of income you receive as a payout) on your tax return.

giving life
insurance

Turn your life insurance into a gift bonanza

WANT TO SAVE EVEN MORE ON ESTATE TAXES? Give away your life insurance policy. Why? Consider this: When you die, the beneficiaries named in your life insurance policy will get the proceeds (the face value of the policy). And while they won't have to pay income tax on that money, if you owned your policy, the proceeds from it will be included in your total taxable estate. If, like most folks, the net value of your estate is less than $1.5 million (as of 2004), estate taxes will not apply to you. But if you add the proceeds from your life insurance (which, in many cases, can be several hundred thousand dollars), your estate may be pushed into taxable territory.

But you can avoid this taxing situation by giving your insurance policy to someone else. There are two ways to do this. One is by setting up an **irrevocable life insurance trust**. In this case, a trust owns the policy and a trustee pays the premiums from money you deposit in the trust. You, meanwhile, set the terms: Do you want the proceeds paid to your heirs immediately upon your death, or paid out over a specified time period?

Another option is to give your policy to your heirs. This is a less expensive and less complicated alternative, as there are legal costs and paperwork associated with setting up a trust. When you give the policy to your heirs, however, they won't necessarily have to pay the premiums: You can still pay those with money you "gift" to them annually.

No matter whom you give your life insurance policy to, you will still be insured by the policy, and your named beneficiaries will still reap the proceeds upon your death. And whichever method you choose, you will have achieved the same goal: moving the policy's proceeds out of your estate so it won't be subject to estate taxes.

ASK THE EXPERTS

The face value of my life insurance policy is $500,000. If I give this policy to my son, won't I get zapped with gift tax? And could this end up being more than the estate taxes he would pay if he inherited it?

Good question. The gift tax on a life insurance policy is not calculated on the face value (in this case, $500,000), but on its cash value—how much you'd get if you cashed the policy in today, minus any outstanding loans taken against the policy. For most people, the cash value is substantially lower than the face value. (For term life insurance policies, which have no cash value, the gift amount for tax purposes is the amount you paid in premiums this year.) So, in most cases, the gift tax incurred when transferring a term or cash-value insurance policy is markedly lower than the estate taxes that would be due after your death.

I'm 55 years old. I'd like to transfer ownership of my life insurance policy that I've held for the past 10 years. Are there any restrictions I should know about?

Not really. But each policy varies, so read the fine print. A warning: If you should die within three years of your policy transfer, the switch won't work. That means the policy proceeds will still be included in your estate and, depending on the size of your estate, be subject to estate tax. This reversal occurs only with policies in which ownership is transferred from you to another party. However, if you were to buy a new policy today and name someone else as the owner, there is no three-year waiting period.

now what do I do?

Answers to common questions

My husband and I gave $22,000 to each of our four grandchildren. Can we deduct these gifts on our income taxes?

Sorry, but no. You can only claim a tax deduction for gifts made to charities. If this seems unfair, remember that the IRS has already given you a tax break by allowing you to remove that $22,000 from your estate, thereby lowering its taxable value. And don't forget, your grandchildren don't have to pay taxes on it when they receive it.

My wife is not a U.S. citizen. Can we still use the unlimited marital deduction to transfer my assets to her tax free before I die?

Unfortunately, no. To take full advantage of that deduction, your spouse must be a U.S. citizen. However, for cases like yours, the IRS does give you something of a break. If your spouse is not an American citizen, you can gift that spouse up to $100,000 per year, instead of the annual $11,000 you can give everyone else.

Does the unlimited gift-tax exclusion for educational expenses cover just college tuition?

Not exactly. You can use the exclusion to pay for tuition at other types of schools as well, such as boarding school, private elementary school, or law school. However, in all cases you are limited to tuition payments only. Room and board, books, and other fees don't qualify; but you could use the annual $11,000 gift-tax exclusion to pay for those items.

Last year, my wife and I gave our son $25,000. We now realize this is $3,000 more than we are allowed to give gift-tax free each year. Who will have to pay the tax on that money—him or us?

In the great land of gifting, taxes are paid by the one who has given the gift—not the recipient. However, you and your wife probably don't owe any taxes at this time either. Each taxpayer is entitled to an estate- and gift-tax credit. (In 2004, it's worth $345,800.) This credit is equal to the amount of tax that would be owed on an estate worth over $1.5 million. Throughout your lifetime, any gift tax you owe (such as on the extra $3,000 given to your son) is subtracted from your total credit. You can continue to cut into this credit until you've used it all up. It is only at that point that you'll have to shell out any actual tax payments. In the meantime, however, you must fill out a gift-tax return with the IRS for all gifts that exceed the annual $11,000 exclusion.

Why should I worry about paying estate taxes? Wasn't that tax repealed a few years ago?

Not exactly. Estate taxes were not abolished by the Federal Tax Act of 2001. What the law did was steadily raise the amount of assets you can pass on without incurring any estate tax. For the years 2002 and 2003, you could leave up to $1 million in assets and your heirs would not have to pay estate taxes. For 2004 and 2005, the amount is raised to $1.5 million. For the years 2006 to 2008, the estate amount is $2 million. For the year 2009, you can leave an estate of up to $3.5 million tax free. In the year 2010 there will be no estate taxes levied, regardless of the amount of your estate. But in 2011, the law "sunsets," meaning it reverts back to 2002. In other words, only estates up to $1 million will be tax free. Anything over that amount, and your heirs will pay estate taxes. Yes, this makes estate planning difficult. This is why estate lawyers advise to always factor in some kind of estate tax.

 **N**OW WHERE DO I GO?!

WEB ADDRESSES	PUBLICATIONS
www.ssa.gov Home of the Social Security Administration	**Benefits Handbook** By Stanley A. Tomkiel III
www.SaveWealth.com Offers information on taxes and how to choose a qualified estate-planning attorney.	**The Retirement Savings Time Bomb** **. . . And How to Defuse It** By Ed Slott
www.nafep.com The National Association of Financial Estate Planning covers changes in gift-tax exemption charts and includes capital gains tax information.	**The Women's Estate Planning Guide** By Zoe M. Hicks, Esq.
	The Baby Boomer Financial Wake-Up Call: It's Not Too Late to Be Financially Secure! By Kay R. Shirley, Ph.D., CFP

glossary

Activities of Daily Living (ADLs)—These activities trigger long-term care insurance benefits. Examples include eating, transferring (in and out of bed, chairs), dressing, bathing, and using the toilet.

Address—To Internet users, there are two types of addresses—Web page and e-mail. Web page addresses (called URLs) look like this—http://www.bn.com. And e-mail addresses look like this—info@bn.com.

Adjusted Gross Income (AGI)—This is a tax term for all of your income (salary, interest, dividends, retirement income, etc.), adjusted for certain items, like contributions to IRAs and self-employed retirement plans, alimony payments, deductible student-loan interest, and deductible moving expenses. The significance? It's used in many calculations to figure out if you can take certain deductions and credits.

Annuity—This is an investment that guarantees income payments to its owner for the owner's lifetime. When an investor buys an annuity (using after-tax dollars), his investment grows tax deferred until he begins to withdraw money from the account. Of course, there's a cost to the guaranteed income and the tax-deferred growth. Commissions, administrative fees, surrender charges, and early withdrawal penalties often make annuities a wise investment for only a small number of people.

Asset—This is essentially anything of value. Examples include your bank accounts, investments, house, and jewelry.

Assisted Living—This hybrid housing alternative is similar to independent-living arrangements and also contains elements of a nursing home, such as help with activities of daily living (ADLs).

BCC (Blind Carbon Copy)—An e-mail setting that lets you send a copy of a message to someone secretly—so the other recipients can't see the e-mail address.

Beneficiary—The person who benefits from being named on an investor's retirement account (IRA, 401(k), SEP IRA) or life insurance policy: If the owner dies, the money transfers to the beneficiary named.

Bond—Essentially a loan from a government or company to an individual, a bond is a promise to pay a fixed amount of interest for the use of someone else's money for a fixed period of time. For this reason, bonds are known as fixed income investments.

Bookmark—You can't slip a card between Web pages to keep your place, but your Web browser can keep a record of sites you want to return to. These records are called Bookmarks—or Favorites, or Favorite Places, depending on your browser.

Broker—Whether you make your own decisions or listen to an adviser, you need a broker to buy stocks and bonds. If you come up with your own ideas, discount brokers can execute the trades for you. If you want someone to do the research for you, you need a full-service broker. Their commissions generally are higher than those of discount brokers.

Browser—A program used to view (and hear) the information on the World Wide Web. The most popular are Microsoft Internet Explorer, Netscape Navigator and Netscape Communicator.

Byte—A byte is the basic unit of storage on your computer. It's so small that most of the files you'll see are measured in thousands of bytes (kilobytes, or KB) or millions of bytes (megabytes or MB).

Capital Gains Tax—When stocks increase in value, the profit you make is called a capital gain. If you sell the stock, you owe tax—the capital gains tax—on the difference between the price you paid for it and the price you sold it for. This tax generally applies to any investment you sell for more than you paid. If you hold your investment for more than one year, the capital gain is considered long-term and is taxed at better rates than your other income. If you hold it for less than one year, it's considered short-term and is taxed just like your other income.

Chat—On a computer, chat doesn't involve your voice at all. It's a typed conversation between two or more people, all of whom are online at the same time. Chats can take place in chat room sites or by using a program like AOL's Instant Messenger.

Chronic Illness—An illness that lasts more than three months is considered to be chronic. More than 90 million Americans live with chronic illnesses such as arthritis, cancer, diabetes, and heart disease.

Clinical Depression—A feeling of pervasive sadness that must be treated with medication and/or therapy. Other symptoms include a loss of interest in daily activities and a marked change in appetite or sleeping patterns. Depression can be triggered by other chronic illnesses common in later life such as diabetes, stroke, and arthritis.

Cookie—A little text file that many Web sites save on your hard disk, used to help the site recognize you as you move from page to page.

Collateral—This is any asset you pledge to the bank (or other money lender) in return for a loan. If you default (don't repay the loan), the collateral is given to the bank to help satisfy your debt.

Continuing Care Retirement Communities (CCRCs)—These communities combine independent living, assisted living, and nursing home care all in one location, allowing seniors to "age in place" without moving every time their situation changes.

Credit Shelter Trust—Also known as a Bypass Trust or an A-B Trust, this estate-tax-saving trust allows the first $1 million of a person's estate to flow into a trust for the kids (or other heirs), rather than going right to the surviving spouse. Any assets over the $1 million flow to the surviving spouse. When the spouse dies, the $1 million exclusion will be used again, so a total of $2 million will escape tax.

Default—A choice made by the software program when you, the user, don't respond. Defaults are built into all software programs to make them easier and faster to use.

Defined Benefit Pension Plan—This is a fancy name for a retirement plan that pays longtime employees a specific amount of money (a defined benefit) each month once they retire. It's highly desirable, since employees don't have to contribute any money to this plan in order to benefit from it.

Defined Contribution Pension Plan—This is a fancy name for a 401(k) or similar plan. These plans generally rely on you (the employee) to make regular (defined) contributions to your own account, which grows tax-deferred until you need the money, usually after retirement. The amount you receive at retirement depends on how much you invested in the plan over the years and how well the account's investments performed.

Dependents—People who depend on you, usually your children or elderly parents, for financial support. In order to qualify as a dependent, the person must meet certain requirements (income, citizenship, relationship and others). Claiming dependents can be a tax saver (as long as your AGI is less than $259,800 if you're single, $328,500 if you're married).

Desktop—In Windows, the Desktop is everything you see on the screen before you open any programs or folders. It consists of the My Computer and other icons and any wallpaper pictures you may have.

Dialog Box—Any box that appears and asks you to click on a button or enter a word is called a dialog box. It's called that because Windows wants you to respond in some way—like two people talking.

Dividend—An added bonus to some stock investments, dividends are a part of a company's profits returned to the shareholders. Mutual funds also pay dividends to their shareholders, based on the income of the fund's underlying stocks and bonds.

Domain—The Internet's address system is based on domains. Where postal addresses have ZIP codes and street names, the Internet uses Top Level Domains (TLDs) and domain names. The top level domain is the cluster of letters after the last period in a Web address (.com, .org, .gov, .edu, and so on). A domain name consists of a name and the TLD—such as fi.edu or bn.com

Download—To take a file, Web page, or e-mail message from a computer on the Internet and deliver it to your own computer.

Early Retirement—The traditional retirement age is 65. If you retire before this time, it's considered early retirement. The amount you receive in a pension and/or Social Security benefits may be affected if you take early retirement. You may also be penalized if you withdraw money from an IRA or a 401(k) plan before age 59½.

E-Mail—Typed messages that are delivered from one computer to another over the Internet.

Equity—1. This is another term for stocks. 2. If you're talking about home equity, this is the difference between what you could sell your home for and the current amount of your mortgage.

Estate Planning—Not something only for the superrich, estate planning is the process of planning for the disposition and administration of assets at a person's death (or in the event of mental or physical incapacity).

Estate Tax—If you die with "too much" money and you don't qualify for certain deductions, the IRS will levy estate taxes on the assets you leave behind. You're allowed to leave as much as you want to your spouse or to charity, and the first $1 million beyond that is also exempt. But after that, this hefty tax—37 percent to 55 percent—kicks in.

Executor—This is the person named in a will to handle all of a deceased person's financial affairs, or estate.

FAQ—Frequently asked questions or FAQs should be your first port of call at a new Web site. They are Web pages that tell you information you need to know about a Web site or the subject the Web site is dedicated to.

File—All the information you see on a computer, and all the programs you run, are stored in files.

File Format—Because a computer file can contain programs, pictures, text, or sounds, each type of information is stored in a different way. This is called the file format, and it's usually referred to by its "file **extension**." A picture from the Internet may be in GIF or JPEG format, for example.

Fixed Income—See Bond.

Folder—In Windows, as in a regular office, files are stored in folders. Using Windows Explorer, you'll see little manila folder icons tucked away in most drives. Double-click on them, and they will open up to reveal the files inside.

Fund Manager—A mutual fund's main decision maker. The manager's ability to pick stocks and read the economy is often a key factor in a fund's success.

Home Page—Home refers to a number of things: 1. the first page you see in when you start your Web browser; 2. the first page you see when you visit a Web site; and 3. your personal page on the Web.

Host—Any computer you can reach on the Internet is called a host.

HTML—Hypertext markup language—the code used to write Web pages. It creates text formatting, defines the position of graphics, and creates links to other Web pages.

HTTP—Hypertext transfer protocol. The code that browsers use to transfer Web pages appears in the address field of your browser. Sometimes you'll see an s at the end—https://—which shows that the page you're viewing is on a super-secure server.

Independent Living—These retirement communities are geared toward mobile older folks who want to remain independent but who want to live in a community with their peer group, and may want the convenience of prepared meals, housekeeping, and activities.

Individual Retirement Account—See IRA.

Inflation—This measures how fast the prices of goods and services are rising.

Institutes for Learning in Retirement—These courses, offered on many college campuses to students age 50 and older, are inexpensive and don't have tests or grades. Topics range from Chaucer and computers to history and yoga.

Interest—The amount a lender charges a borrower for the use of his money. Simple interest is based on the principal only. Compound interest, on the other hand, is based on the amount of principal, plus any accumulated interest.

Internet—A massive network of computers that stretches across the whole world.

Internet Service Provider (ISP)—Any company that can hook you up to the Internet is called an Internet Service Provider. These companies usually provide a phone number for your computer to dial, or provide special customer service.

IRA—Investors use Individual Retirement Accounts to stash money for retirement. Interest and dividends that are earned in this type of account aren't taxed until you withdraw the money, usually after retirement.

IRS—The Internal Revenue Service is the governmental body that's in charge of collecting taxes on behalf of the federal government.

Itemized Deductions—Mortgage interest, real estate taxes, charitable contributions, and state income taxes add up to significant tax reductions. Even though it can mean a more complicated tax return, it's often more beneficial than taking the standard deduction.

Keogh—A type of individual retirement fund for those who are self-employed.

Life Insurance—In exchange for annual payments (or "premiums"), a life insurance company will issue a contract (or "policy") that promises to pay a fixed amount when the policy's owner dies. The payment is made to the person listed in the policy as the beneficiary. Term policy premiums stay low for a fixed number of years (usually 5 to 30), then usually rise dramatically if the owner wants to keep the policy in place. Permanent policy premiums start out higher than term premiums, but stay level for the owner's entire lifetime. Permanent policies also have a savings component, called the cash value, which builds over time.

Link—Web pages contain text or graphics that you can click on, taking you to other Web pages. These are called links—and are often underlined or surrounded with blue lines.

Living Trust—Living trusts are like wills, but they allow any assets held by the trust to avoid probate and pass directly to your heirs. However, they are often more costly to create than wills and more burdensome to manage during your lifetime.

Long-Term Care Insurance—This type of health insurance picks up costs that traditional health insurance does not, such as an extended stay in a nursing home or nursing care in your own home. This type of insurance is expensive, especially if you buy it when you're 60 years of age or older.

Long-Term Capital Gain—See Capital Gains Tax.

Lump Sum Distribution—At retirement, you can often withdraw the entire balance of your retirement plan in one single payment. Frequently, retirees then put this "lump" into a rollover IRA.

Medicaid—This health insurance provides free coverage for low-income people of any age. You may also qualify for Medicaid if you are disabled.

Medicare—This health insurance for people age 65 and older is offered by the federal government at low or no cost. Medicare doesn't cover all medical costs, and it pays only a portion of the costs of many services. Medicare has two parts: Part A and Part B. (See Medicare Part A and Medicare Part B.)

Medicare Part A—This hospital insurance covers hospital stays, hospice care, and some home health care.

Medicare Part B—This medical insurance covers most doctors' services, medical equipment, and supplies.

Medigap—This supplemental insurance policy fills the "gap" between the medical coverage that Medicare offers and the coverage that many people need. There are 10 standard medigap policies. Each policy, ranging from letter A to letter J, offers additional benefits.

Modem—The gadget that lets your computer talk to computers on the Internet.

Municipal Bond—Issued by state and local governments, municipal (or "muni") bonds generally are not taxed by the federal government. Since this makes them more attractive, munis can get away with paying investors less than other bonds.

Mutual Fund—When an investment company pulls together many investors to pool their money to buy stocks and bonds, a mutual fund is born, and its investors (or shareholders) are able to diversify better than if they were on their own.

Nursing Homes—These long-term care (or skilled nursing) facilities provide 24-hour support for people with chronic and long-term illnesses who can't live independently. They generally provide a full range of services, including daily nursing care, and dietary and therapeutic assistance.

Online Service—Online services are Internet Service Providers that add special private sites and services that regular Internet users can't get to. America Online, CompuServe and the Microsoft Network are three examples.

Pension Plans—See Defined Benefit Pension Plan and Defined Contribution Pension Plan.

Portfolio Manager—A generic term for someone who makes investment decisions for a large pool of money. Examples of companies that hire portfolio managers include mutual funds, insurance companies, pension plans, and banks' trust departments.

Power of Attorney—A written, legally binding document that gives another person the right to make financial or health decisions on your behalf.

Probate—This is the long and winding road heirs must follow through the court system to carry out the deceased's wishes, as made known in his or her will.

Prospectus—Used most frequently by mutual funds, this little booklet (required to be given to potential investors) includes information about the fund's management, objectives, and past performance.

Required Minimum Distributions—These are the withdrawals the IRS requires you to start taking out of your IRAs, annuities, and other retirement accounts once you reach age 70½. Failure to comply will cost you a 50 percent penalty!

Return On Investment—Also known as ROI. When you invest money in stocks, bonds, and mutual funds, you eventually want to get back more than you invested. The amount you get back, over and above your beginning investment, is called your return. If you divide your return by the amount you originally invested, you can calculate the percentage of your "return on investment." Knowing this percentage helps you compare investments.

Reverse Mortgage—This is the payment(s) the bank makes to you, based on the equity in your home. It doesn't need to be repaid until your house is sold, typically after your death, when your heirs sell the home. Common types of reverse mortgages include Tenure Reverse Mortgages, where you receive monthly payments for the rest of your life, regardless of how long you live; Term Reverse Mortgages, where you receive a fixed number of monthly payments; and a Line of Credit Reverse Mortgage, where you receive a specified line of credit that you may draw on.

Risk—Your investment might not increase as you expect it to; or worse, it could end up losing money. This possibility is known as risk. Investors accept risk, however, because they believe that the possible payoff (or "return") will ultimately be worthwhile.

Rollover—At retirement, you can take the money from your 401(k) in one lump-sum distribution. Trouble is, you'll owe taxes on that money—all at once. A smarter strategy is to *roll over* the money directly from your former employer's 401(k) plan into an IRA. That way, you'll still have complete control of the funds, yet the money will continue to grow tax-deferred until withdrawal.

Roth IRA—Named after the senator who invented it, the Roth IRA is an individual retirement account that doesn't allow an upfront deduction (like a traditional IRA). Instead, this nifty IRA uses after-tax dollars to fund it, so when the money is withdrawn during retirement, the investor doesn't have to pay tax on the money it earned over the years.

Savings Bond—Issued by the U.S. government, savings bonds are sold at most banks and cost half of their face value. They don't make interest payments, per se, but they do increase in value each year. When you receive the face value at maturity, the difference between what you originally paid for it, and the amount you get back, is considered interest income and is taxed on your federal income tax (but not your state income tax).

Search Engine—A program that searches for things on the Web—usually the general content of Web pages; but some search engines specialize in videos, sound files or even news stories.

SEP IRA—A Simplified Employee Pension (SEP) allows self-employed people and small business owners to set up retirement plans that work like a 401(k), but aren't subject to as many rules, regulations, and administrative details. These plans generally allow self-employed individuals to sock away up to 20 percent of their net business income, up to a maximum of $40,000 per year.

Server—Any computer on a network that provides a service is a server. The types of services available on the Internet include e-mail handling, Web data and file transfer.

Short-Term Capital Gain—See Capital Gains Tax.

SIMPLE IRA—Geared toward small business owners who want to contribute to their employees' retirement accounts, Simple IRAs are similar to 401(k) plans, but they're not as popular as SEP IRAs.

Spam—Also known as bulk e-mail, direct e-mail or just plain junk, spam is the derogatory name given to unwanted e-mail.

Spousal Benefits—Social Security benefits that your spouse (or ex-spouse) can collect, based on your earnings. These are usually one-half of your benefit.

Standard Deduction—If you don't list out (or "itemize") your deductions on your income tax return, you can take the standard deduction, which is a minimum fixed deduction amount that all taxpayers are entitled to deduct.

Stock—This is a type of investment that represents ownership in a company.

Survivor Rights—When you die, your spouse will get at least half the pension benefit that you were receiving. If you pick the single-life option, however, you waive your survivor rights.

Taxable Income—This is the amount of your total income that you have to pay tax on, after all possible deductions have been taken.

Tax Credit—Certain credits are allowed to offset your tax bill, dollar for dollar. Examples of these credits include a $600 credit for each child under age 17; income tax paid to a foreign government; and education credits for certain college costs for you or your children.

Tax-Deferred—Interest, dividends, and other gains aren't subject to taxation in these types of accounts until the owner withdraws money from them, usually after retirement.

Title Bar—The title bar is the top part of a window. At the left, it contains the name and icon of the program, and at the right, three buttons that you use to minimize, maximize or close the window.

Tool Bar—A bar with buttons or icons. Used to set graphic functions such as changing fonts and type size.

Trust—This is a very general term that describes a wide range of vehicles used to own property. Trusts generally don't save money on taxes. They're used mostly when someone wants to put restrictions or parameters on how their property is used, managed, and distributed to others.

URL—Stands for Uniform Resource Locator, a horribly long-winded way of saying Web address.

Will—This basic legal document specifies who gets your money and property after you die. It also names the person who will handle your affairs (the executor, or the estate administrator), and names a guardian for any minor children.

Yield—Refers to the percent of income an asset is paying. A stock's yield is called the "dividend yield," and is calculated by taking the amount of dividend the company pays and dividing it by the stock's price. A bond's "yield to maturity" is a little trickier to calculate—it's usually given to you by a broker. It represents the bond's total return, if you hold it until it matures.

Zip File—To make computer files quicker to send over the Internet, people compress them into zip files. Before they can use them again, they have to uncompress them—like putting one of those dried-out sponges into water and watching it grow.

index

about the authors

Hope Egan is a financial planner as well as a certified public accountant. She has provided retirement, income tax, and investment guidance to individuals, small business owners, and large corporations, such as Ernst & Young and LaSalle National Trust. She was a contributing editor to **Barnes & Noble Basics** *Saving Money* (formerly published as *I Haven't Saved a Dime, Now What?!*).

Barbara Wagner has written about retirement, debt, and—yes—those dreaded budgets for the past 10 years. She recently wrote "The Retirement Revolution" for Fidelity Investment's magazine for 401(k) participants. Her work has also appeared in *Business Week* and *Working Mother*, and she is the author of four consumer finance books, including a guide to 401(k)s and IRAs.

Matthew James is the pseudonym of a professional computer-technology writer who, after much coaxing, agreed to come down from his technological mountaintop to help real people understand how to use a computer. To do this he agreed to keep his explanations simple and clear-cut and to write in plain English. James has written for some of the most esteemed high-tech publications, including *PC World*, *Computers Made Easy*, *CNET*, and *ComputerUser*. He reminds us that "while the computer is not your friend, if you can tell it what to do, it will do as it is told."

Barnes & Noble would like to thank the following experts for their help in preparing this book: James Dreggors of Dreggors, Rigsby, and Teal; Thomas Lee, President of the Senior Resources of America; and Randall J. Marshall of Marshall Law Office, PA.

Barbara J. Morgan Publisher
Barb Chintz Editorial Director
Leonard Vigliarolo Design Director
Wynn Madrigal Senior Editor
Emily Seese Editorial Assistant
Leslie Stem Design Assistant
Della R. Mancuso Production Manager

Picture Credits

Artville 17, 18, 24, 25, 45, 48, 58, 82, 86, 94, 100, 116, 151, 153, 224, 227; **Comstock** 33; **Corbis** 80 Bob Krist, 147, 163, 168, 189; **Corbis Stock Market** 1 (left) Ariel Skelley, 1 (right) H. Armstrong Roberts; **Digital Stock** 3, 9, 14, 15, 20, 31, 41, 44, 49, 50, 52, 56, 64, 71, 75, 79, 89, 102, 113, 119, 127, 130, 139, 159, 203, 210, 212, 217, 221, 222; **Robert Milazzo** 167; **PhotoDisc** 7, 8, 12, 16, 23, 29, 30, 32, 34, 36, 42, 51, 63, 68, 72, 80, 81, 84, 85, 93, 104, 115, 120, 122, 142, 148, 154; **Sally Mara Sturman** cover, 164, 185, 192, 197, back cover; **SuperStock** 178